WORDS TO KNOW
FIRST GRADE
SIGHT WORDS

fly

Brighter Child®
Carson Dellosa Education
Greensboro, North Carolina

W9-BSC-517

Brighter Child®
Carson Dellosa Education
PO Box 35665
Greensboro, NC 27425 USA

Printed in the USA • All rights reserved.   ISBN 978-1-4838-4933-1
01-042191151

Table of Contents

For Parents and Caregivers

This book will help your child learn to read and write 100 of the most commonly used words in the English language. Memorizing these words, or knowing them "by sight," will form a strong foundation for your child as he or she grows as a reader.

What Are Sight Words?

Sight words are words that children see often in books, on signs, at school, and everywhere! Sometimes called *high-frequency words*, *instant words*, or *core words*, these are the short words that make up much of what we read. It is estimated that the same 100 words or so make up more than half of all the words that students are expected to read. If that seems hard to believe, look at a page from any book. How many of the words on that page are common words like *and*, *the*, *I*, *or*, and *that*?

Some sight words cannot be sounded out using phonics rules. Or, they rely on rules that your child will learn later in school. Imagine trying to sound out each letter in words like *could* and *know*. It doesn't work very well! Memorizing these words frees your child to concentrate on sounding out words that follow more predictable patterns.

Some sight words can be sounded out, but they are so common that it is an advantage to memorize them. Words like *has*, *went*, and *ask* appear frequently in children's books. With a little practice, your child will learn to read them at a glance.

Why Is It Important to Learn Sight Words?

Learning to read the words in this book "by sight" will greatly benefit your child as a new reader. First, learning sight words develops **confidence**. When your child looks at a book and already recognizes many words, he or she is more likely to keep reading. Second, knowing sight words promotes **reading comprehension**. Since your child will already know many words, he or she can focus on new words that are important to the meaning of a text. Finally, learning sight words will help your child develop **speed and fluency**. With so many words already memorized, reading is full speed ahead!

How Will This Book Help My Child Learn Sight Words?

This book features 100 sight words for first graders arranged in 10 sections according to their level of difficulty and some shared spelling and meaning patterns. Dip into the activities at any point—it is not necessary to go from front to back. The **tracing**, **writing**, **word recognition**, and **spelling activities** are short, predictable, and easy to do, providing the repeated practice that will help your child remember each word. A **review** at the end of each section includes sentences and stories. A complete set of **flash cards** is provided for hands-on practice.

How Can I Help My Child Learn Sight Words?

The activities in this book are a great starting point for helping your child learn sight words. Try these ideas for even more practice.

☐ Cut out the flash cards at the back of this book. See page 281 for creative suggestions for using the cards.

☐ Look for sight words on signs, menus, junk mail, and everywhere!

☐ Focus on one sight word. How many times can your child find it as you read a picture book together? Praise your child for reading the word!

☐ Use magnetic letters to spell sight words on the fridge or on a cookie sheet.

☐ Play hangman to reveal a sight word. Or, play tic-tac-toe, writing sight words in place of X and O.

☐ Write a sight word on a strip of construction paper. Staple it in a loop around your child's wrist. How many times during the day can your child spy the word?

☐ Use letter stamps, play dough, scented markers, sidewalk chalk, or other fun supplies to write sight words.

☐ Rainbow-write! Write a sight word at a large size. Have your child use crayons to trace it in every color of the rainbow.

☐ Choose several sight words. Use them to write a sentence or a story together. Try trading short notes, texts, or e-mails that use sight words.

☐ Write sight words with your finger in a cookie tray filled with salt or dry rice.

☐ Print out a story. Provide two or three highlighters of different colors, assigning a sight word to each color. Ask your child to highlight sight words in the story using the colors.

☐ Write sight words on masking tape pieces stuck to the floor around the room. Call out a sight word. Can your child run to the word and stand on it?

My List of 100 Words

Make a check mark beside each word you know how to read. If you need help, find the word's pages and practice again.

☐ **about** (pages 128–129)

☐ **after** (pages 224–225)

☐ **again** (pages 226–227)

☐ **an** (pages 8–9)

☐ **any** (pages 60–61)

☐ **as** (pages 10–11)

☐ **ask** (pages 112–113)

☐ **been** (pages 98–99)

☐ **book** (pages 50–51)

☐ **brother** (pages 254–255)

☐ **by** (pages 34–35)

☐ **could** (pages 202–203)

☐ **done** (pages 94–95)

☐ **each** (pages 142–143)

☐ **every** (pages 206–207)

☐ **face** (pages 76–77)

☐ **fish** (pages 140–141)

☐ **fly** (pages 138–139)

☐ **friend** (pages 182–183)

☐ **from** (pages 168–169)

☐ **give** (pages 170–171)

☐ **going** (pages 102–103)

☐ **grow** (pages 144–145)

☐ **had** (pages 20–21)

☐ **hand** (pages 68–69)

☐ **happy** (pages 174–175)

☐ **has** (pages 44–45)

☐ **head** (pages 72–73)

☐ **her** (pages 38–39)

☐ **hers** (pages 42–43)

☐ **him** (pages 36–37)

☐ **his** (pages 40–41)

☐ **house** (pages 104–105)

☐ **how** (pages 114–115)

☐ **just** (pages 192–193)

☐ **kind** (pages 246–247)

☐ **know** (pages 260–261)

☐ **last** (pages 218–219)

☐ **leave** (pages 208–209)

☐ **left** (pages 90–91)

☐ **let** (pages 16–17)

☐ **live** (pages 96–97)

☐ **love** (pages 26–27)

☐ **man** (pages 242–243)

☐ **many** (pages 62–63)

☐ **may** (pages 46–47)

☐ **money** (pages 204–205)

☐ **more** (pages 198–199)

- [ ] **morning** (pages 234–235)
- [ ] **name** (pages 126–127)
- [ ] **new** (pages 22–23)
- [ ] **next** (pages 86–87)
- [ ] **night** (pages 232–233)
- [ ] **now** (pages 216–217)
- [ ] **of** (pages 12–13)
- [ ] **old** (pages 48–49)
- [ ] **once** (pages 200–201)
- [ ] **open** (pages 166–167)
- [ ] **over** (pages 92–93)
- [ ] **part** (pages 52–53)
- [ ] **pet** (pages 18–19)
- [ ] **please** (pages 258–259)
- [ ] **present** (pages 180–181)
- [ ] **pretty** (pages 176–177)
- [ ] **put** (pages 14–15)
- [ ] **ride** (pages 194–195)
- [ ] **round** (pages 156–157)
- [ ] **saw** (pages 64–65)
- [ ] **second** (pages 230–231)
- [ ] **shoe** (pages 100–101)
- [ ] **should** (pages 256–257)
- [ ] **show** (pages 66–67)
- [ ] **sister** (pages 252–253)
- [ ] **slow** (pages 196–197)
- [ ] **small** (pages 146–147)
- [ ] **some** (pages 148–149)
- [ ] **soon** (pages 222–223)
- [ ] **stop** (pages 190–191)
- [ ] **table** (pages 178–179)
- [ ] **take** (pages 150–151)
- [ ] **thank** (pages 172–173)
- [ ] **them** (pages 124–125)
- [ ] **then** (pages 118–119)
- [ ] **these** (pages 70–71)
- [ ] **thing** (pages 250–251)
- [ ] **think** (pages 248–249)
- [ ] **time** (pages 220–221)
- [ ] **today** (pages 228–229)
- [ ] **under** (pages 154–155)
- [ ] **walk** (pages 88–89)
- [ ] **want** (pages 24–25)
- [ ] **water** (pages 152–153)
- [ ] **went** (pages 74–75)
- [ ] **were** (pages 78–79)
- [ ] **what** (pages 122–123)
- [ ] **when** (pages 120–121)
- [ ] **who** (pages 116–117)
- [ ] **wish** (pages 164–165)
- [ ] **woman** (pages 244–245)
- [ ] **would** (pages 130–131)

as

of

put

let

pet

had

new

want

love

an

READ the word. SAY it out loud.

That is an eel.

TRACE and WRITE the word.

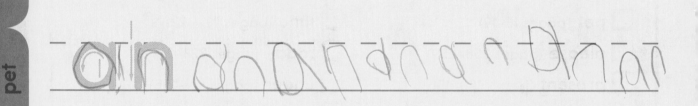

FIND the word. Circle **an**.

SPELL the word. On each plant, circle the letters in **an**.

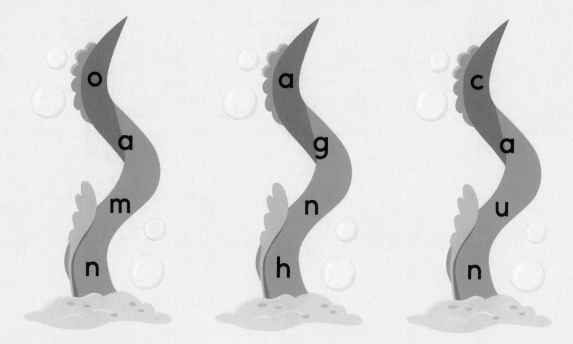

an
as
of
put
let
pet
had
new
want
love

an
as
of
put
let
pet
had
new
want
love

as

READ the word. SAY it out loud.

I am busy **as** a bee.

TRACE and WRITE the word.

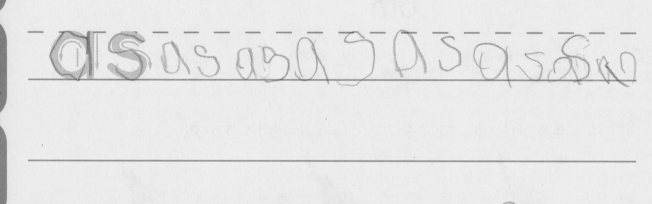

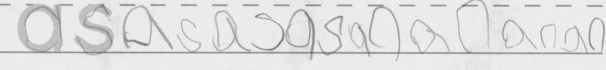

WRITE as in each sentence. Draw a line to the picture that matches.

I am clever _____ a fox.

I am slow _____ a snail.

I am angry _____ a bear.

I am hungry _____ a goat.

FIND the word. Draw lines through **as** to see if you won!

as	an	ask
am	as	act
sat	at	as

an	ask	as
am	act	as
sat	at	as

an
as
of
put
let
pet
had
new
want
love

an

as

of

put

let

pet

had

new

want

love

of

READ the word. **SAY** it out loud.

I ate a bowl of cereal.

TRACE and **WRITE** the word.

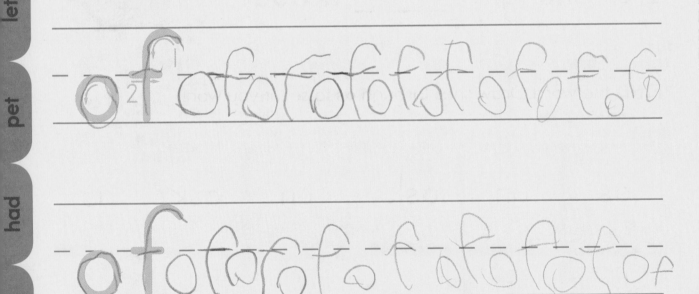

FIND the word. Color the spaces with **of**.

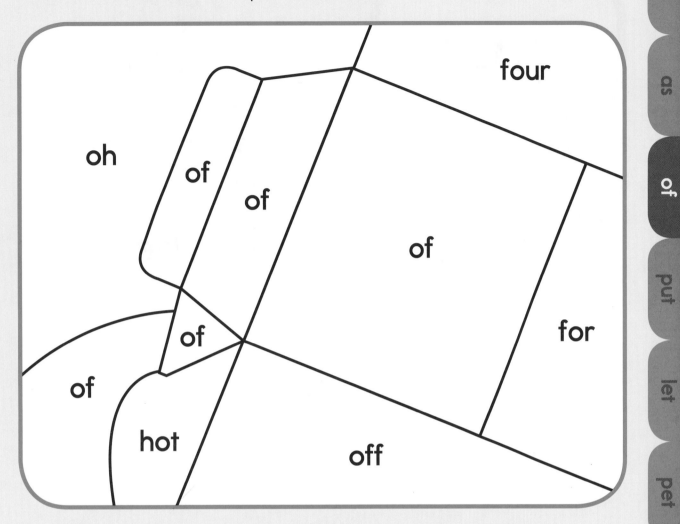

SPELL the word. Write the missing letters.

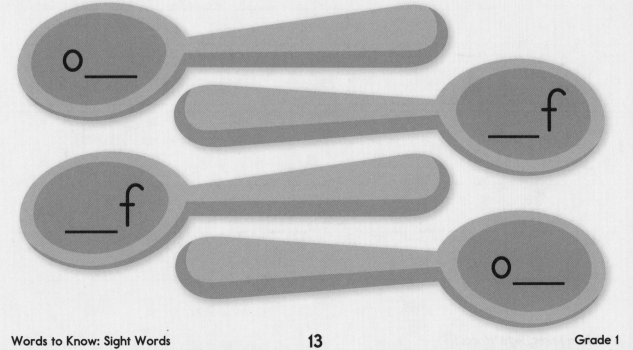

an
as
of
put
let
pet
had
new
want
love

an
as
of
put
let
pet
had
new
want
love

put

READ the word. **SAY** it out loud.

Put the candy in the jar.

TRACE and **WRITE** the word.

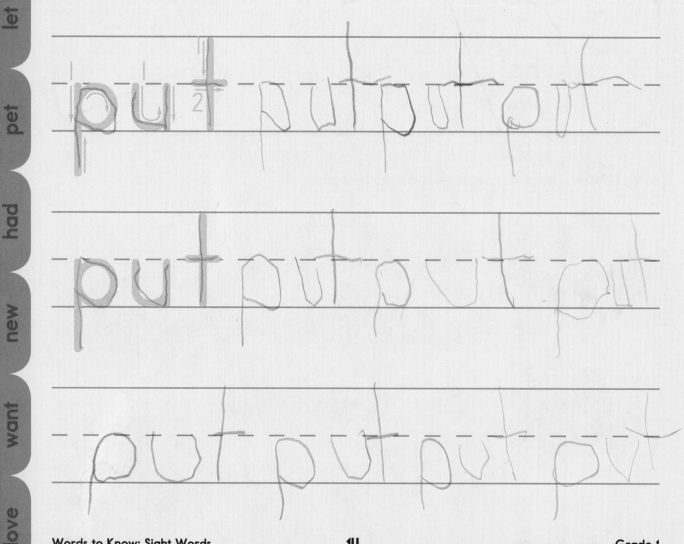

FIND the word. Color the candy with **put**.

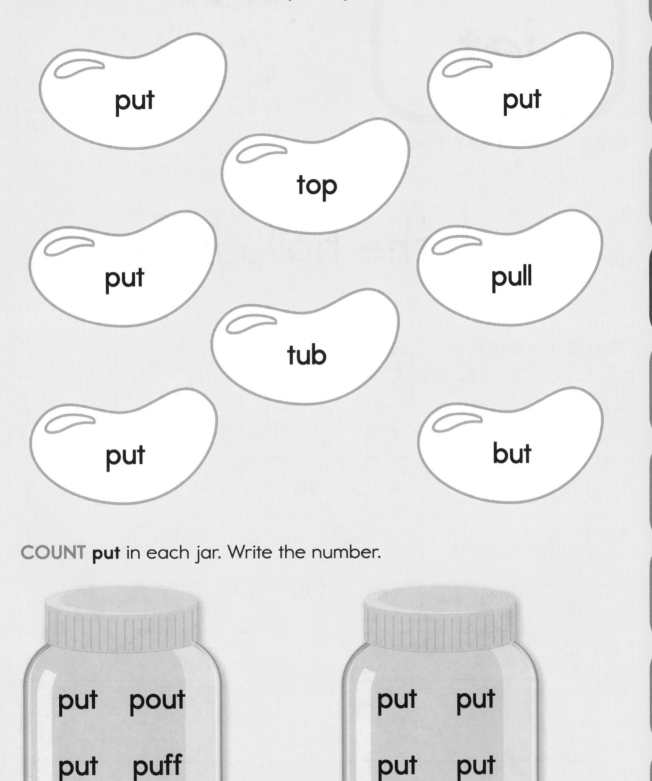

put

put

top

put

pull

tub

put

but

COUNT put in each jar. Write the number.

put	pout
put	puff
pet	put

put	put
put	put
pat	pot

_____

_____

an
as
of
put
let
pet
had
new
want
love

let

READ the word. **SAY** it out loud.

Let the balloon go.

TRACE and **WRITE** the word.

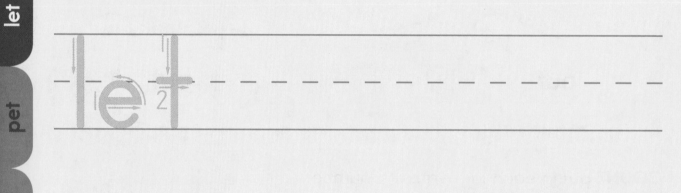

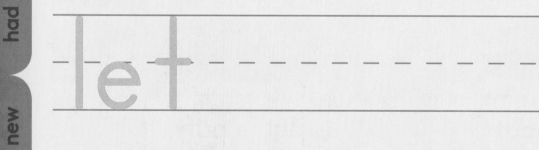

FIND the word. Circle **let**.

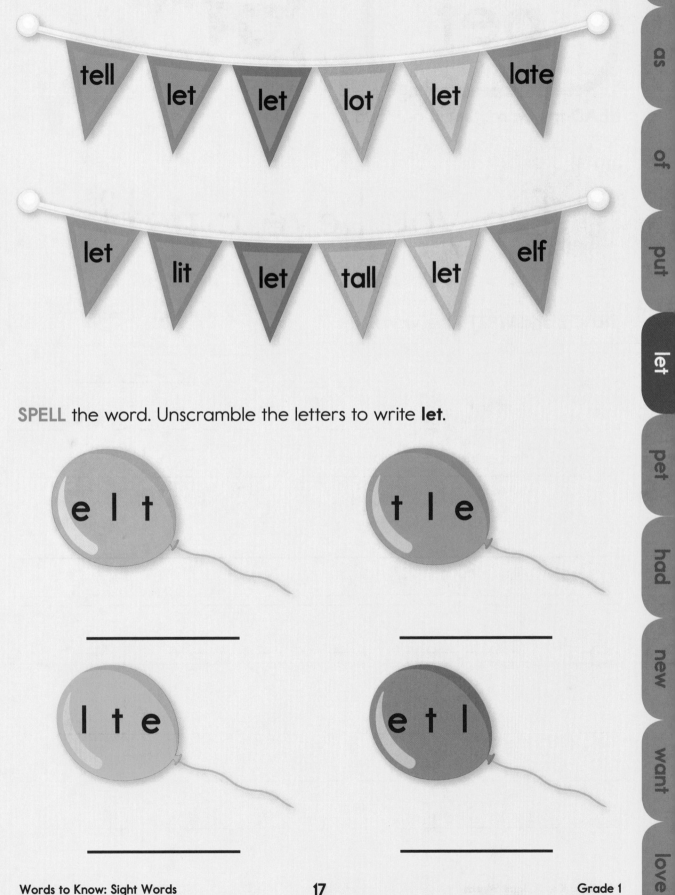

tell

let

let

lot

let

late

let

lit

let

tall

let

elf

SPELL the word. Unscramble the letters to write **let**.

e l t

t l e

_____

_____

l t e

e t l

_____

_____

pet

READ the word. SAY it out loud.

Do you have a pet?

TRACE and WRITE the word.

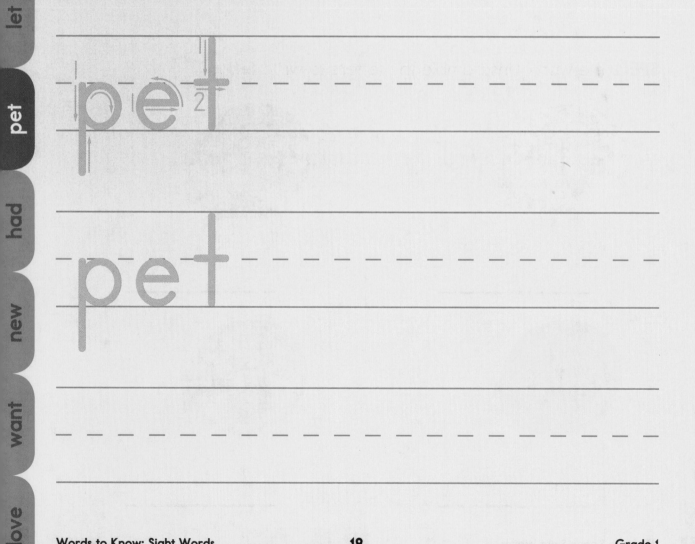

pet

pet

FIND the word in the puzzle. Look → and ↓.

r	p	e	t	s
k	p	e	t	p
p	p	e	t	e
e	d	y	k	t
t	z	m	q	k

SPELL the word. Match the letters in **pet**.

19

an
as
of
put
let
pet
had
new
want
love

had

READ the word. **SAY** it out loud.

I had pizza for lunch.

TRACE and **WRITE** the word.

FIND the word. Color the spaces with **had**.

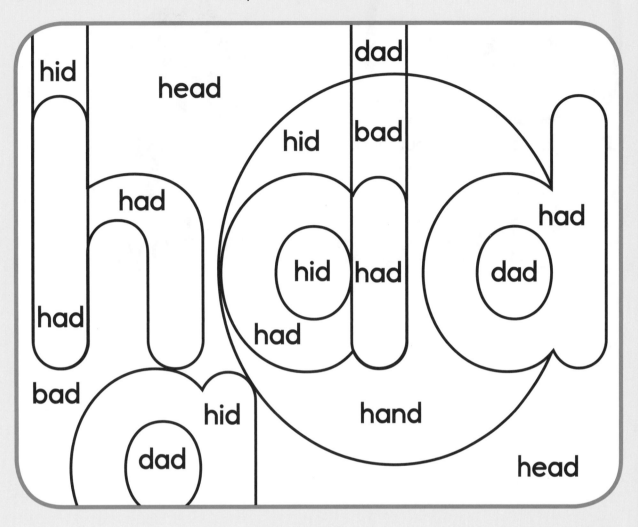

SPELL the word. Write the missing letters.

h__d   __ad   __a__   h__d

an

as

of

put

let

pet

had

new

want

love

an
as
of
put
let
pet
had
new
want
love

new

READ the word. SAY it out loud.

I have a new toy.

TRACE and WRITE the word.

FIND the word. Color the spaces with **new**.

WRITE new under the things that are new.

_____   _____   _____

_____   _____   _____

an
as
of
put
let
pet
had
new
want
love

as
an

as

of

put

let

pet

had

new

want

love

READ the word. **SAY** it out loud.

I want to see outer space.

TRACE and **WRITE** the word.

FIND the word. Color the stars with **want**.

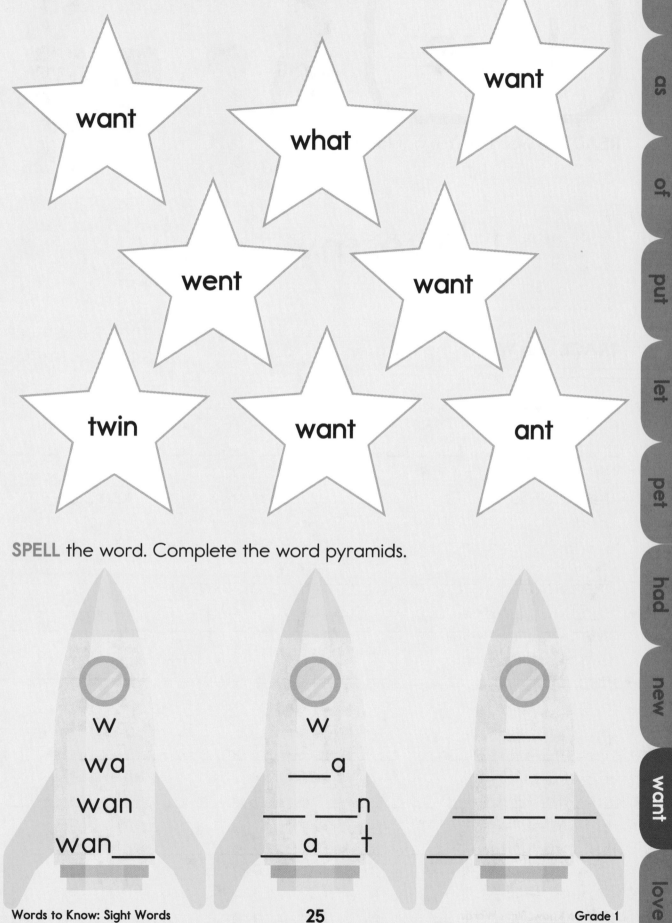

want

what

want

went

want

twin

want

ant

SPELL the word. Complete the word pyramids.

w
wa
wan
wan___

w
___a
___ ___n
___a___ t

___
___ ___
___ ___ ___
___ ___ ___ ___

an
as
of
put
let
pet
had
new
want
love

an
as
of
put
let
pet
had
new
want
love

READ the word. **SAY** it out loud.

I love my family.

TRACE and **WRITE** the word.

WRITE love in each sentence. In each heart, draw something you love.

I _____ .

I _____ .

I _____ .

SPELL the word. Unscramble the letters to write **love**.

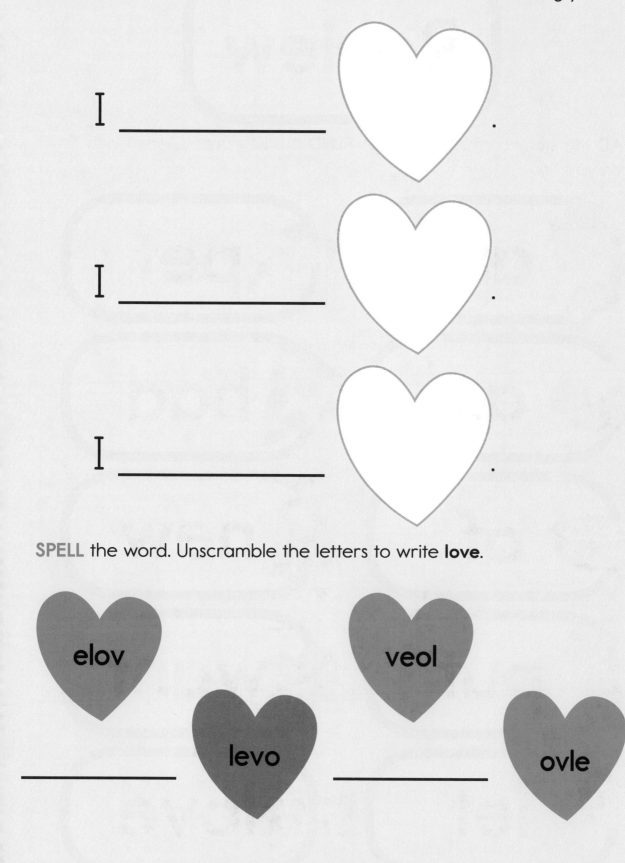

elov

veol

levo

_____

_____

ovle

_____

_____

an
as
of
put
let
pet
had
new
want
love

an
as
of
put
let
pet
had
new
want
love

Review

READ the story on the next page. FIND the 10 words. Circle each word you find.

an

pet

as

had

of

new

put

want

let

love

Review

What Pet?

"Dad," I said, "I want a new pet."

"What kind of pet?" asked Dad.

"I want a pet that I have never had before."

"So, not a stuffed animal. You have lots of those," Dad joked.

"No! I want a real animal. An animal that will let me pet it as much as I want."

"So, not a rhino," Dad teased.

"No! I want a pet that I can put in my lap."

"How about a puppy?" asked Dad.

"Yes! I would love to get a puppy!"

an
as
of
put
let
pet
had
new
want
love

Review

words to finish the sentences.

want	put	pet	an	of

Joey has a _____ goldfish in a bowl.

I drank a glass _____ lemonade.

Do you _____ to play a game?

Sari _____ on her hat and gloves.

Would you like a pear or _____ apple?

I _____ the rabbit's soft fur.

Dad has a fear _____ high places.

an as of put let pet had new want love

Review

WRITE words to finish the sentences.

as	let	had	new	love

I got _____ clothes for school.

Will your mom _____ you come over?

This worm is _____ long _____ my hand.

I told Grandma that I _____ her.

We _____ chicken for dinner.

_____ this string hang down.

January begins a _____ year.

an
as
of
put
let
pet
had
new
want
love

an
as
of
put
let
pet
had
new
want
love

Review

SORT the words. WRITE each word on a cone.

want pet an put as let had new of love

_____

_____

_____

_____

_____

_____

_____

_____

_____

**Words with
2 Letters**

**Words with
3 Letters**

**Words with
4 Letters**

Review

WRITE a word in the puzzle to complete each sentence.

want pet an put as let had new of love

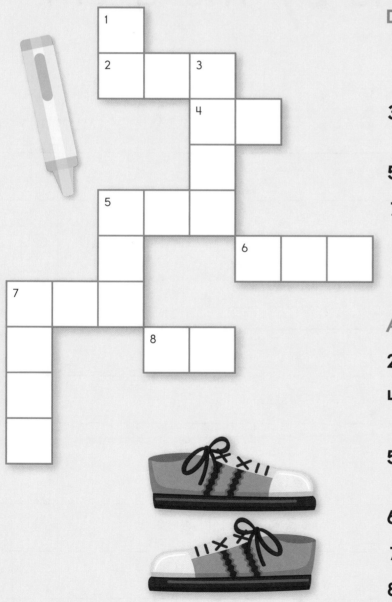

DOWN

1. Do you see ___ orange crayon?

3. What movie do you ___ to watch?

5. Izzy is my ___ iguana.

7. Mom and Dad ___ me.

ACROSS

2. I need ___ shoes.

4. Come as soon ___ you can.

5. I ___ a dollar in my pocket.

6. We ___ fun last week.

7. Please ___ the dog out.

8. This is a book ___ stories.

by

READ the word. SAY it out loud.

The doll is by the drum.

TRACE and WRITE the word.

34

FIND the word. Draw lines through **by** to see if you won!

by	be	baby
by	boy	bay
by	bee	bye

by	by	by
bye	bay	boy
baby	be	bee

SPELL the word. Match the letters in **by**.

him

her

his

hers

has

may

old

book

part

by
him
her
his
hers
has
may
old
book
part

him

READ the word. **SAY** it out loud.

I play in the snow with him.

TRACE and **WRITE** the word.

FIND the word. Color the spaces with **him**.

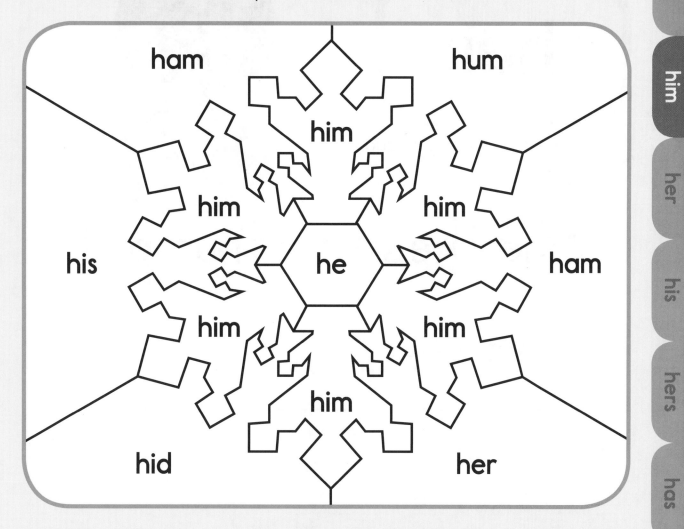

ham

hum

him

him

him

his

he

ham

him

him

him

hid

her

SPELL the word. Unscramble the letters to write **him**.

m i h

i h m

h m i

_____   _____   _____

by
him
her
his
hers
has
may
old
book
part

her

READ the word. **SAY** it out loud.

She likes her trumpet.

TRACE and **WRITE** the word.

FIND the word. Color the spaces with **her**.

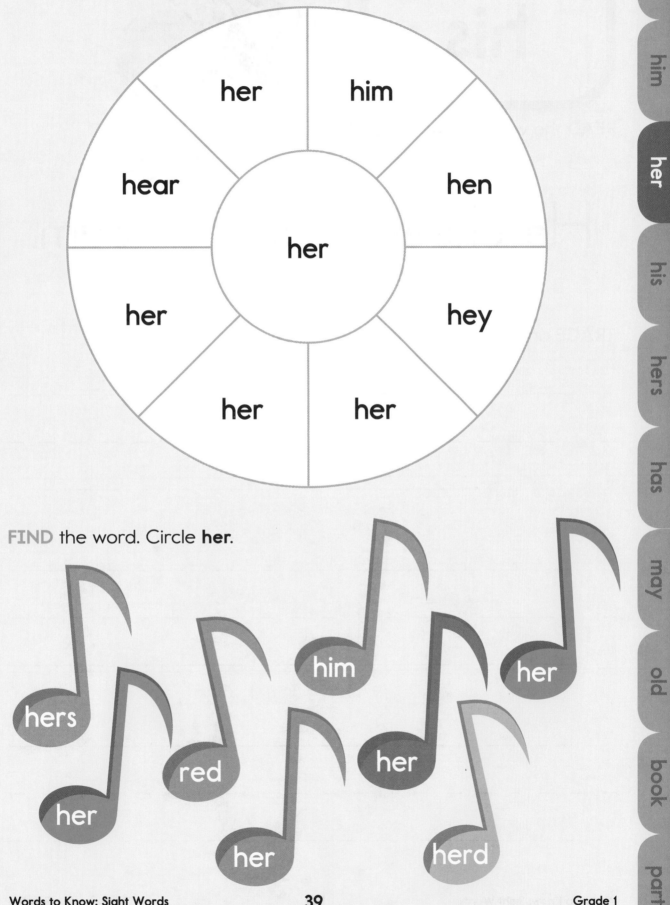

FIND the word. Circle **her**.

by
him
her
his
hers
has
may
old
book
part

Words to Know: Sight Words

39

Grade 1

his

READ the word. SAY it out loud.

He cheers for his team.

TRACE and WRITE the word.

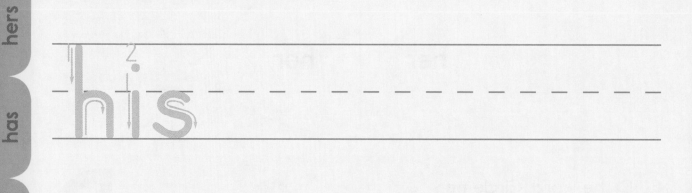

his

his

COUNT the words to see who won. Write the number of times you count **his** under **Home**. Write the number of times you count other words under **Away**.

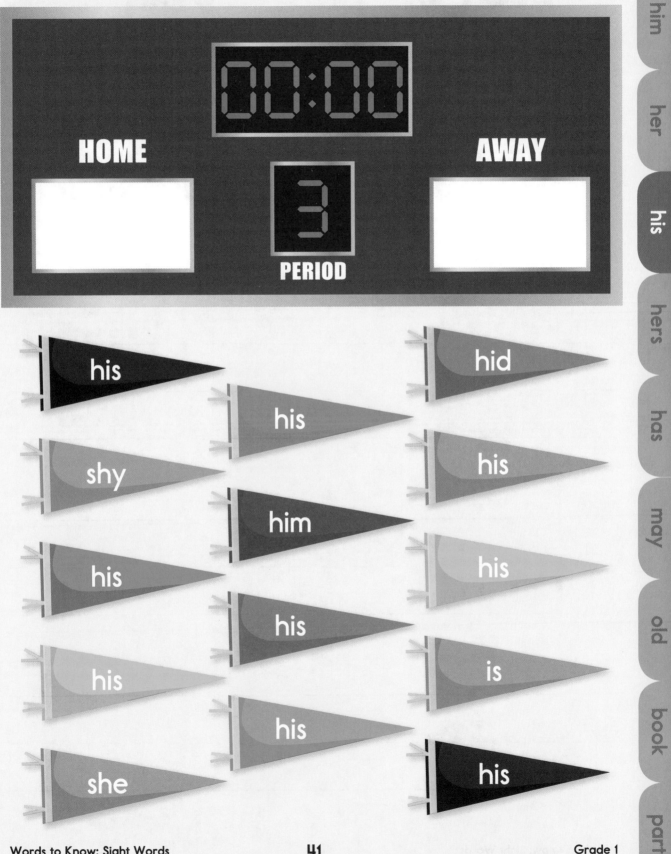

him

her

his

hers

has

may

old

book

part

HOME

AWAY

00:00

3

PERIOD

his

hid

his

shy

his

his

him

his

his

his

is

she

his

hers

READ the word. SAY it out loud.

The yo-yo is hers.

TRACE and WRITE the word.

hers

hers

FIND the word in the puzzle. Look ➜ and ⬇.

s	h	s	s	v
h	e	r	s	h
i	r	k	z	e
l	s	h	w	r
p	h	e	r	s

FIND the word. Circle **hers** in each row.

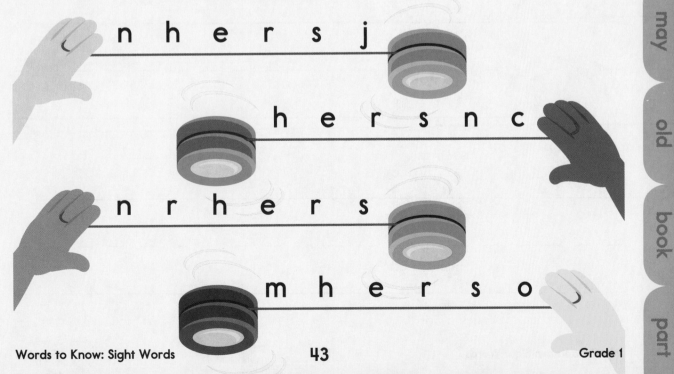

n h e r s j

h e r s n c

n r h e r s

m h e r s o

by

him

her

his

hers

has

may

old

book

part

has

READ the word. SAY it out loud.

The wagon has four wheels.

TRACE and WRITE the word.

has

has

FIND the word. Color the spaces with **has**.

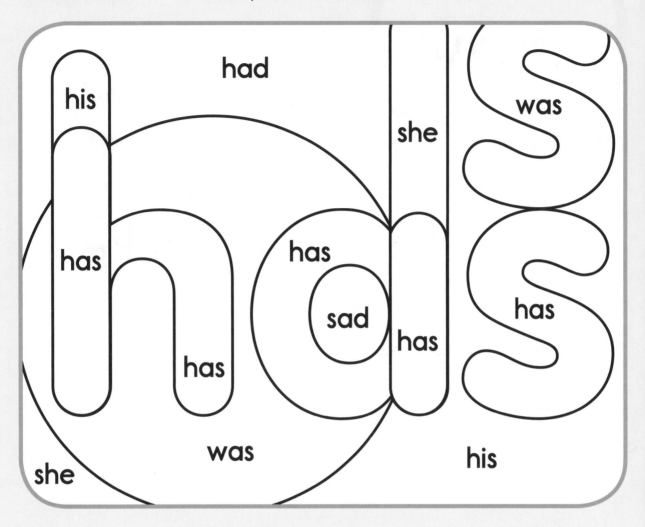

his · had · she · was · has · has · sad · has · has · has · was · his · she

SPELL the word. Circle the missing letter in **has**.

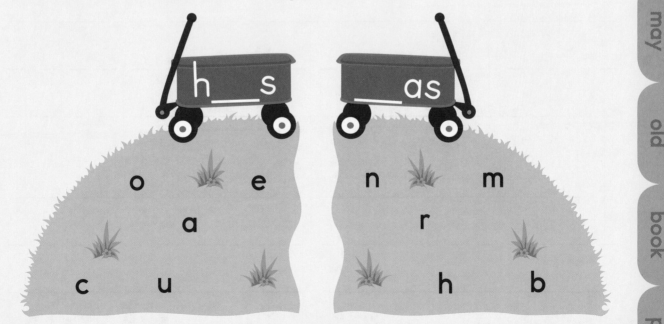

h __ s   __ as

o   e   n   m

a   r

c   u   h   b

may

READ the word. SAY it out loud.

May I have a cupcake?

TRACE and WRITE the word.

may

him
her
his
hers
has
may
old
book
part

FIND the word. Color the gifts with **may**.

may	my	may
mad	man	
may	may	say

SPELL the word. Complete the word pyramids.

m
ma
ma___

m
___a
m___ ___

m
___a
___ ___ y

m
___a
m___ ___

___
___ ___
___ ___ ___

by
him
her
his
hers
has
may
old
book
part

by
him
her
his
hers
has
may
old
book
part

old

READ the word. SAY it out loud.

My teddy bear is old.

TRACE and WRITE the word.

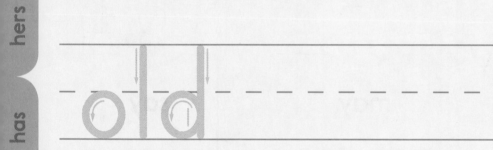

FIND the word. Draw lines from the shoe to **old**.

old

doll

hold

old

old

cold

WRITE old under the things that are old.

_____

_____

_____

_____

_____

_____

by
him
her
his
hers
has
may
old
book
part

by

him

her

his

hers

has

may

old

book

part

book

Run, Rabbit!

READ the word. **SAY** it out loud.

I read this whole book.

TRACE and **WRITE** the word.

book

book

FIND the word. Circle **book**.

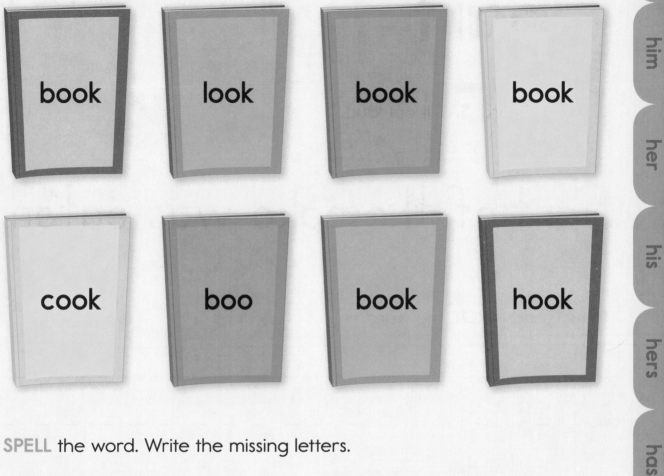

book | look | book | book

cook | boo | book | hook

SPELL the word. Write the missing letters.

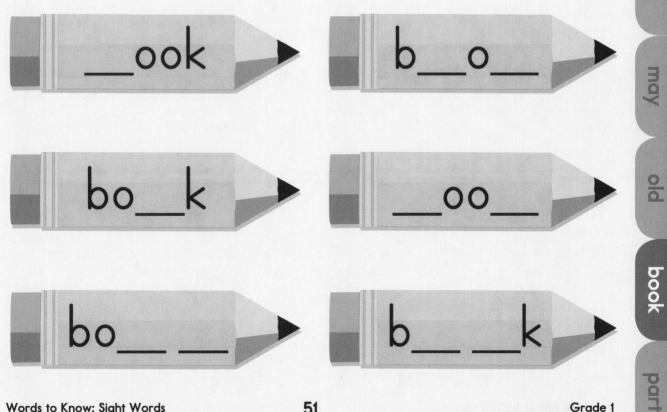

__ook

b__o__

bo__k

__oo__

bo_____

b____k

part

READ the word. **SAY** it out loud.

Part of the cake was eaten.

TRACE and **WRITE** the word.

FIND the word. Circle **part**.

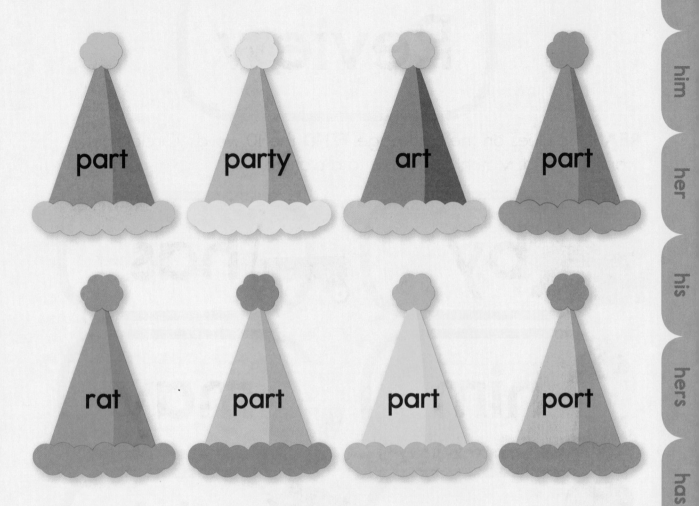

SPELL the word. Write **part** in the puzzle.

by
him
her
his
hers
has
may
old
book
part

by
him
her
his
hers
has
may
old
book
part

Review

READ the clues on the next page. FIND the 10 words. Circle each word you find. Match each clue to a picture.

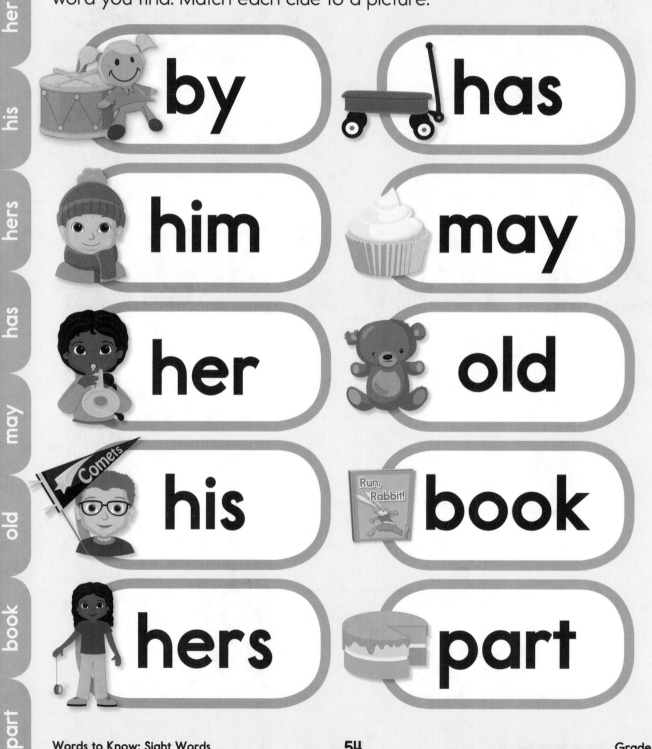

by

has

him

may

her

old

his

book

hers

part

Review

Which Kid?

Her old toy is by her. It has been hers since she was four years old.

He has part of his sweet snack. He may eat the rest later.

He likes to learn about dinosaurs. His teacher gave him a book to read.

by
him
her
his
hers
has
may
old
book
part

Review

WRITE words to finish the sentences.

| book | her | has | by | may |

The elephant _____ two tusks.

Mom asked me to hold _____ purse.

I checked out a library _____.

I sat _____ Marius and Ethan on the bus.

We _____ go to the pool today.

Did you _____ our hotel room?

This book is _____ Barbara Park.

Review

WRITE words to finish the sentences.

| old | him | part | his | hers |

You can have _____ of my cookie.

My brother lost _____ tooth.

I am seven years _____.

Carlos asked me to play with _____.

Bella said the backpack is _____.

This _____ blanket has a hole in it.

Mari got a _____ in the play.

Words to Know: Sight Words   57   Grade 1

by
him
her
his
hers
has
may
old
book
part

Review

COLOR the words that are spelled correctly. WRITE letters to complete the words.

may
him
buk
by
parte
hirs
hers
his
bie
old
oild
hir
has
her
hym
part
hies
book
maye
haz

b__ __k   ha__

p__ __ __ __   __y

h__r__   o__d

__is   ma__

__ __m   __ __r

Review

GRAPH the words. Color one box for each word you count.

his part him by her
old by part may
has may hers has book
part her him part
by
may part has old has

by					
him					
her					
hers					
his					
has					
may					
old					
book					
part					

many

saw

show

hand

these

head

went

face

were

any

READ the word. SAY it out loud.

Are there any eggs left?

TRACE and WRITE the word.

any

FIND the word. Circle **any**.

an | many | am | any
any | zany | any | any

SPELL the word. Unscramble the letters to write **any**.

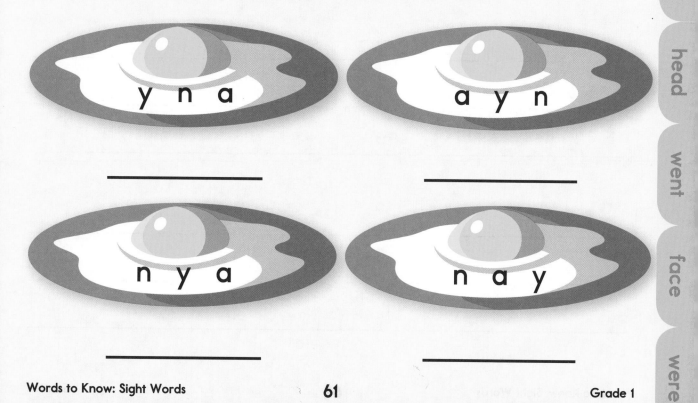

y n a

a y n

_____

_____

n y a

n a y

_____

_____

any
many
saw
show
hand
these
head
went
face
were

any
many
saw
show
hand
these
head
went
face
were

many

READ the word. SAY it out loud.

How many ants are there?

TRACE and WRITE the word.

many

many

COLOR each box with **many**. Match each number to a letter to answer the riddle.

4	any	mane	name	many
3	many	money	mom	pony
2	an	many	only	candy
1	man	and	many	hand

Who comes to a picnic but is never invited?

__ __ __ __ !
1   2   3   4

any
many
saw
show
hand
these
head
went
face
were

any
many
saw
show
hand
these
head
went
face
were

saw

READ the word. SAY it out loud.

I saw a dolphin jump!

TRACE and WRITE the word.

saw

saw

FIND the word. Color the shells with **saw**.

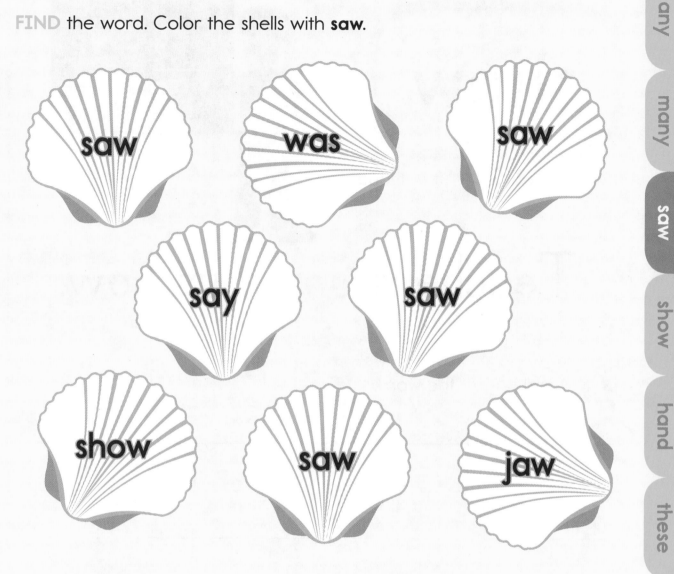

SPELL the word. In each wave, circle the letters in **saw**.

any

many

saw

show

hand

these

head

went

face

were

show

READ the word. SAY it out loud.

Teachers show us how.

TRACE and WRITE the word.

SPELL the word. Match the letters in **show**.

SPELL the word. In each puzzle, connect letters to spell **show**.

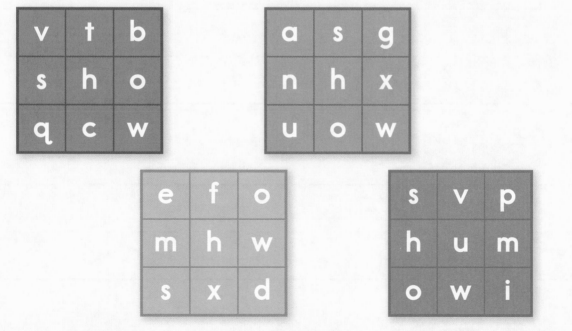

any
many
saw
show
hand
these
head
went
face
were

hand

READ the word. SAY it out loud.

Count fingers on each hand.

TRACE and WRITE the word.

hand

FIND the word. Draw lines from the hand to each **hand**.

hand

hand

and

hand

had

hand

band

WRITE hand to complete each sentence.

Please _____ me the paper.

Raise your _____ high.

Give the singers a big _____.

any

many

saw

show

hand

these

head

went

face

were

any

many

saw

show

hand

these

head

went

face

were

these

READ the word. SAY it out loud.

These are for you.

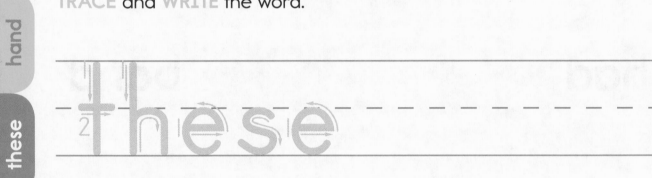

TRACE and WRITE the word.

these

these

FIND the word. Color the spaces with **these**.

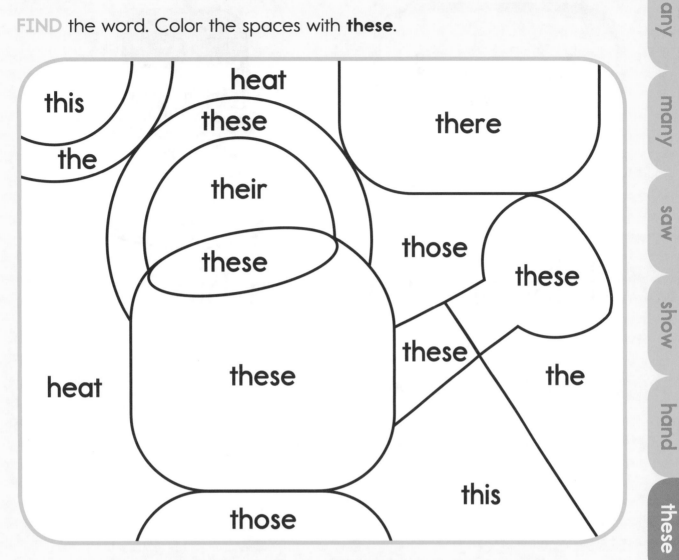

SPELL the word. Circle **these**.

any many saw show hand these head went face were

any
many
saw
show
hand
these
head
went
face
were

head

READ the word. SAY it out loud.

His crown is on his head.

TRACE and WRITE the word.

head

head

FIND the word. Draw a line from the queen to each **head**.

had

head

hand

head

head

herd

SPELL the word. Complete the word pyramids.

___
___e
h___a
___e___d

___
___ ___ ___
___ ___ ___
___ ___ ___ ___

any

many

saw

show

hand

these

head

went

face

were

any
many
saw
show
hand
these
head
went
face
were

went

READ the word. SAY it out loud.

We went on a plane.

TRACE and WRITE the word.

FIND the word in the puzzle. Look ➡ and ⬇.

w	r	w	l	w
e	d	e	b	e
n	q	n	b	n
t	l	t	y	t
m	w	e	n	t

SPELL the word. Write the missing letters.

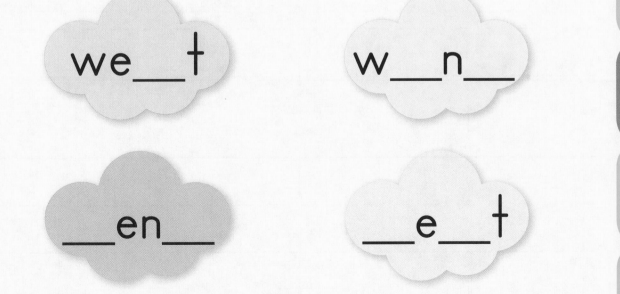

we__t

w__n__

__en__

__e__t

any

many

saw

show

hand

these

head

went

face

were

any

many

saw

show

hand

these

head

went

face

were

face

READ the word. SAY it out loud.

She got her face painted.

TRACE and WRITE the word.

FIND the word. Circle **face**.

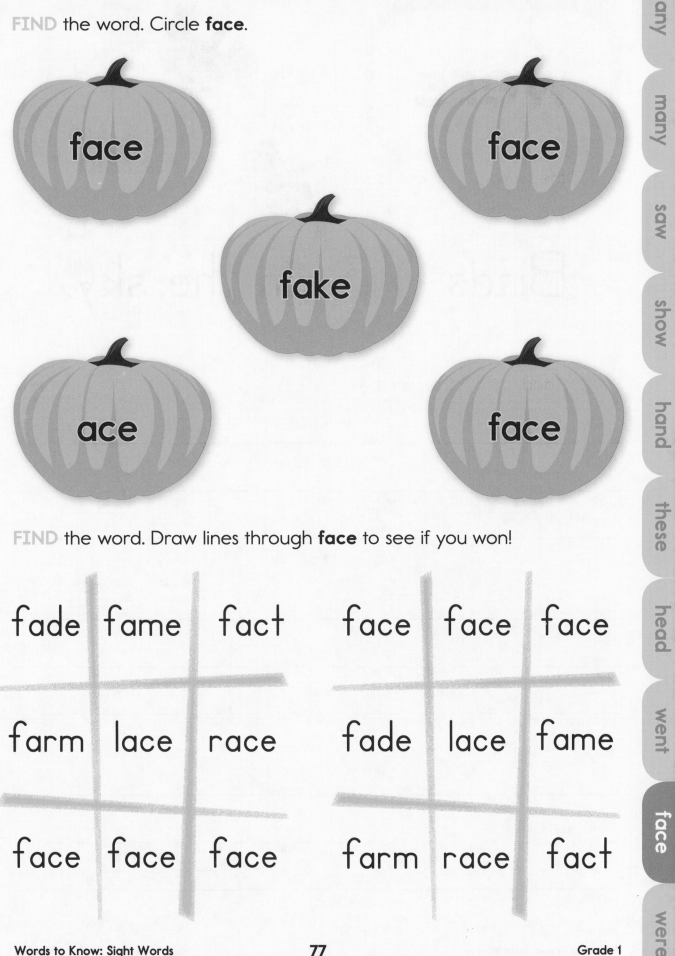

face

face

fake

ace

face

FIND the word. Draw lines through **face** to see if you won!

fade	fame	fact
farm	lace	race
face	face	face

face	face	face
fade	lace	fame
farm	race	fact

any   many   saw   show   hand   these   head   went   face   were

any

many

saw

show

hand

these

head

went

face

were

were

READ the word. **SAY** it out loud.

Birds were in the sky.

TRACE and **WRITE** the word.

were

FIND the word. Color the spaces with **were**.

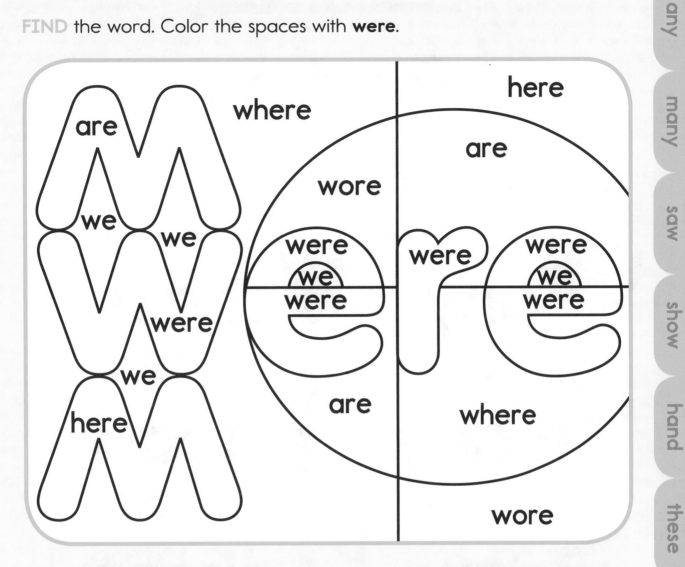

SPELL the word. Unscramble the letters to write **were**.

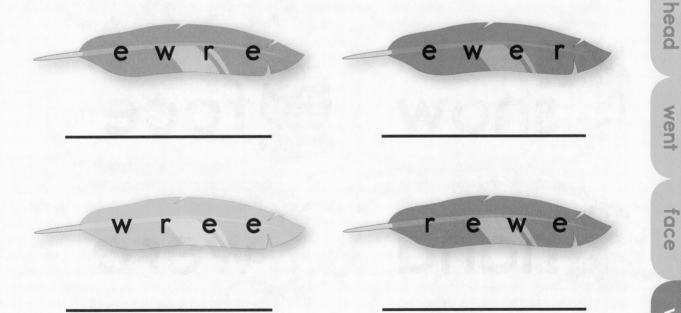

e w r e

e w e r

_____

_____

w r e e

r e w e

_____

_____

any many saw show hand these head went face were

any
many
saw
show
hand
these
head
went
face
were

Review

READ the story on the next page. FIND the 10 words. Circle each word you find.

any
these
many
head
saw
went
show
face
hand
were

Review

Jumping In

Robert saw that many kids were already in. He jumped in, too. The water was cold for these early lessons! Any time now, class would start. Robert watched the teacher show what to do. He put his face in the water. He moved his head to the side to breathe. He dragged his hand through the water as he kicked. He went forward a little bit in the pool. Robert was doing it! He was swimming!

any

many

saw

show

hand

these

head

went

face

were

Review

WRITE words to finish the sentences.

| show | these | face | any | saw |

We _____ a pretty bird.

Anita had a smile on her _____.

_____ snacks are for the party.

Let me _____ you what I made!

Do you have _____ good ideas?

Sam decided to _____ his problem.

We need a hammer and a _____.

Review

any many saw show hand these head went face were

WRITE words to finish the sentences.

hand   were   many   head   went

_____ chickens live in this coop.

Hold the umbrella over your _____.

I held a worm in my _____.

My friends _____ so nice to me!

He _____ to camp last summer.

We are going to _____ home.

Please _____ me the envelope.

Review

FIND the words in the puzzle. Look → and ↓.

~~the~~   ~~face~~   ~~went~~   ~~show~~   ~~hand~~
~~head~~   ~~many~~   ~~were~~   ~~any~~   ~~saw~~

k	w	e	n	t	p	f	r	m	s
h	o	u	w	m	a	n	y	y	j
n	f	v	j	d	p	j	x	q	a
z	a	d	h	r	w	n	t	c	o
b	c	n	t	h	e	s	e	t	f
s	e	b	k	z	r	p	h	c	a
h	j	t	k	e	e	q	d	z	n
o	e	p	f	j	h	a	n	d	y
w	g	r	g	h	e	a	d	d	k
j	k	s	a	w	m	l	j	p	x

any | many | saw | show | hand | these | head | went | face | were

Review

MATCH the words. Use the codes to complete the jokes.

1. head   show ⭐e
2. face   any ⭐r
3. many   head ⭐w
4. show   many ⭐t
5. any   face ⭐a

What do you call an old snowman?

___ ___ ___ ___ ___!
① ② ③ ④ ⑤

1. these   hand ⭐s
2. went   these ⭐w
3. saw   were ⭐e
4. were   saw ⭐v
5. hand   went ⭐a

How do you know that the ocean is friendly? It ___ ___ ___ ___ ___!
① ② ③ ④ ⑤

next
walk
left
over
done
live
been
shoe
going
house

 **next**

READ the word. **SAY** it out loud.

What color comes next?

TRACE and **WRITE** the word.

FIND the word. Circle **next** in each row.

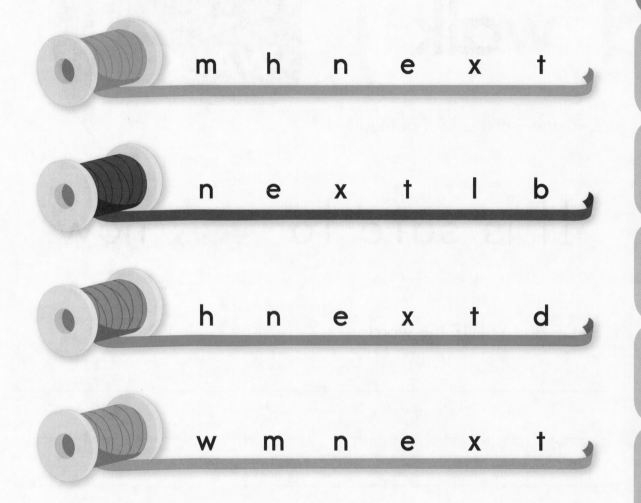

m h n e x t

n e x t l b

h n e x t d

w m n e x t

SPELL the word. Circle **next**.

negst   next   next

nixt   next   neks

next

walk

left

over

done

live

been

shoe

going

house

next
walk
left
over
done
live
been
shoe
going
house

walk

STOP
WALK

READ the word. **SAY** it out loud.

It is safe to walk now.

TRACE and **WRITE** the word.

walk

FIND the word. Color the spaces with **walk**.

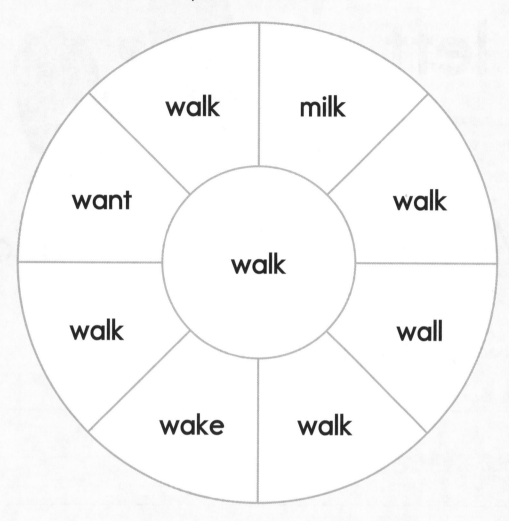

SPELL the word. Complete the word pyramids.

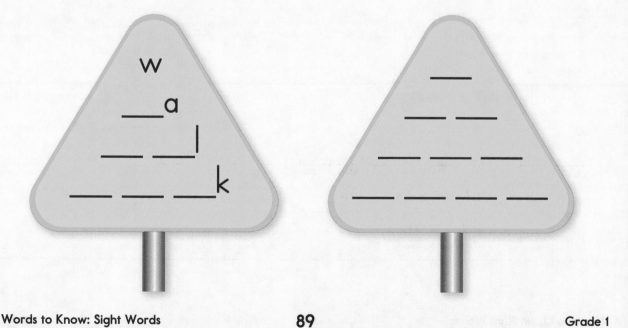

next

walk

left

over

done

live

been

shoe

going

house

left

READ the word. SAY it out loud.

My left mitten is striped.

TRACE and WRITE the word.

left

FIND the word. Circle **left**.

WRITE left to complete each sentence.

Is there any soup _____?

My backpack got _____ behind.

Make the sled turn _____.

91

next
walk
left
over
done
live
been
shoe
going
house

next
walk
left
over
done
live
been
shoe
going
house

over

READ the word. SAY it out loud.

Planes fly over the clouds.

TRACE and WRITE the word.

over

over

FIND the word. Color the spaces with **over**.

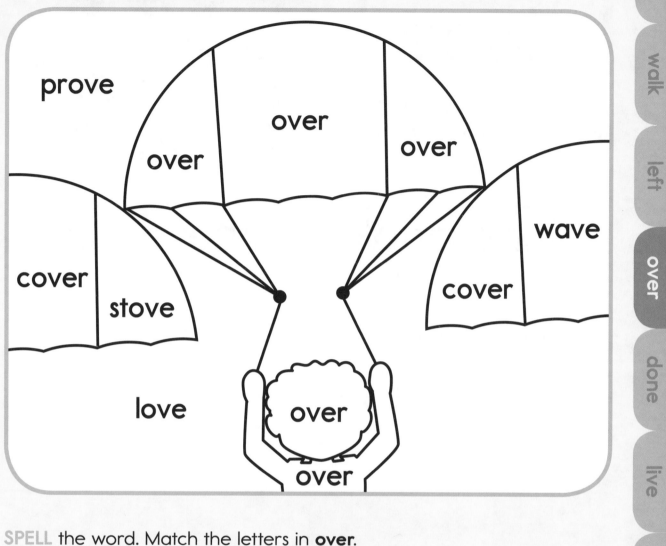

SPELL the word. Match the letters in **over**.

ov

r

ove

ver

o

er

done

READ the word. **SAY** it out loud.

The cookies are done.

TRACE and **WRITE** the word.

done

COLOR each box with **done**. Match each number to a letter to answer the riddle.

	i	p	c	m	h
5	one	done	won	door	den
4	den	phone	zone	done	bone
3	done	gone	don't	ton	come
2	bone	money	dome	won	done
1	come	none	done	one	gone

What is a monkey's favorite cookie?

Chocolate __ __ __ __ __!
    1 2 3 4 5

next walk left over done live been shoe going house

next
walk
left
over
done
live
been
shoe
going
house

live

READ the word. **SAY** it out loud.

Chipmunks live in tunnels.

TRACE and **WRITE** the word.

live

live

FIND the word. Circle **live**.

live   alive   love

live   dive

live   live   life

SPELL the word. In each tunnel, circle the letters in **live**.

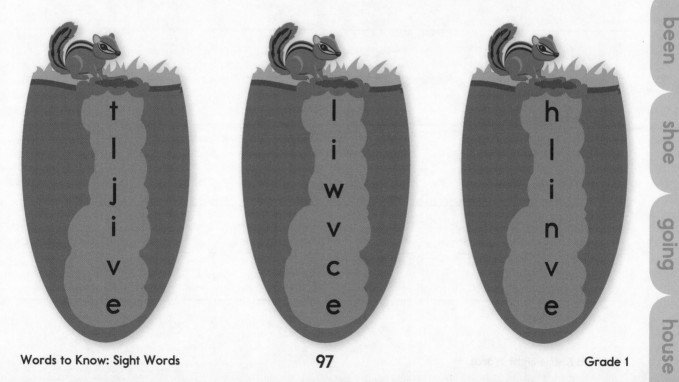

t l j i v e

l i w v c e

h l i n v e

next   walk   left   over   done   live   been   shoe   going   house

next
walk
left
over
done
live
been
shoe
going
house

been

READ the word. SAY it out loud.

We have been at the beach.

TRACE and WRITE the word.

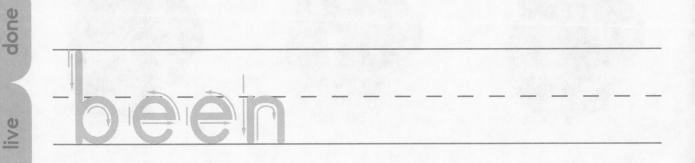

been

been

FIND the word. Color the spaces with **been**.

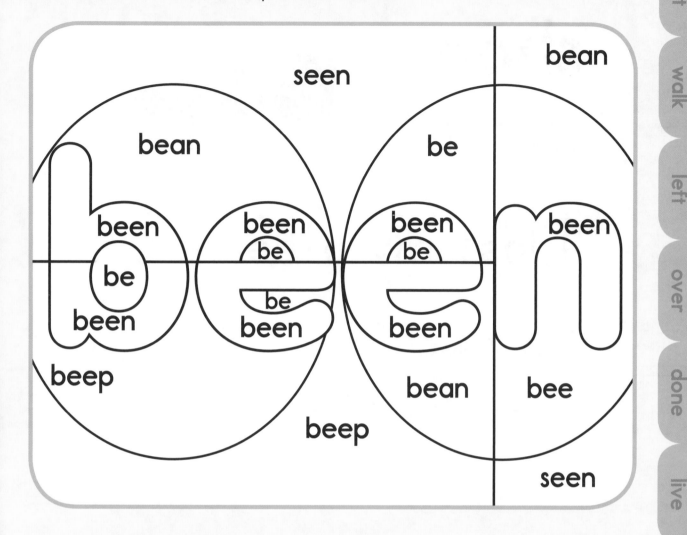

FIND the word. Circle **been** in each ray.

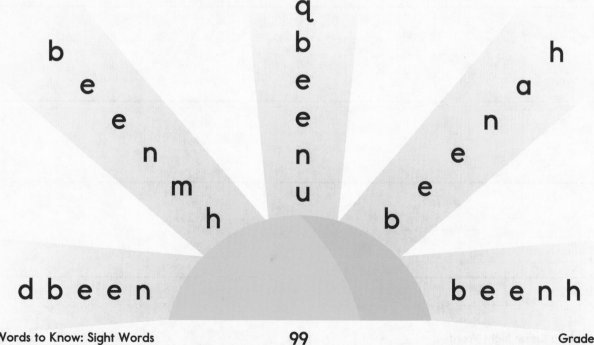

next   walk   left   over   done   live   been   shoe   going   house

next
walk
left
over
done
live
been
shoe
going
house

READ the word. **SAY** it out loud.

I lost my other shoe.

TRACE and **WRITE** the word.

shoe

shoe

FIND the word in the puzzle. Look → and ↓.

s	h	o	e	z
s	q	t	s	s
h	x	h	y	h
o	d	h	o	o
e	s	h	o	e

SPELL the word. Unscramble the letters to write **shoe**.

h e o s

s o h e

_____

o s e h

e s h o

_____

next
walk
left
over
done
live
been
shoe
going
house

next
walk
left
over
done
live
been
shoe
going
house

going

Fay's Farm

READ the word. SAY it out loud.

We are going to the farm.

TRACE and WRITE the word.

going

going

COUNT **going** and write the number on the barn.

next
walk
left
over
done
live
been
shoe
going
house

next
walk
left
over
done
live
been
shoe
going
house

house

READ the word. SAY it out loud.

Come to my house.

TRACE and WRITE the word.

house

house

FIND the word. Circle **house**.

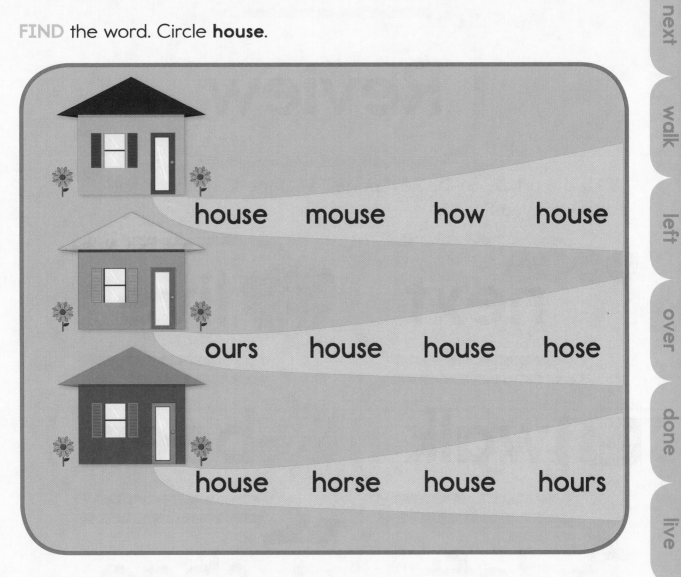

house   mouse   how   house

ours   house   house   hose

house   horse   house   hours

SPELL the word. Connect the letters in **house**.

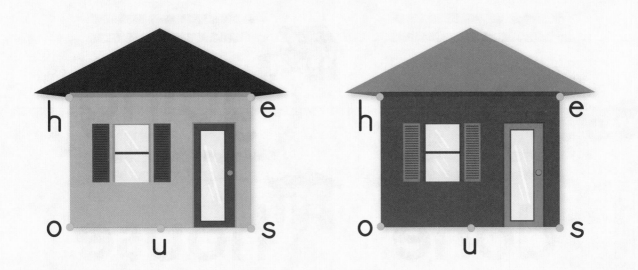

Words to Know: Sight Words   105   Grade 1

next
walk
left
over
done
live
been
shoe
going
house

Review

READ the article on the next page. FIND the 10 words. Circle each word you find.

next

live

walk

been

left

shoe

over

going

done

house

Review

Hermit Crabs

The next time you are by the ocean, look for a shell that seems to walk by itself. It could be a live hermit crab going across the sand. Hermit crabs have ten legs and two claws. The left claw is larger. It can be used as a weapon.

Hermit crabs have soft bodies that need protection. So, they look for an old shell that they can use over again as a house. Just like you need a new shoe when your foot grows, hermit crabs need larger shells as they get bigger. When they are done with one shell, they look for a new one. Hermit crabs have been seen fighting each other for better shells.

next walk left over done live been shoe going house

Review

WRITE words to finish the sentences.

over	been	going	next	shoe

I am _____ to win the race!

It has _____ a long day.

I need to tie my _____.

Is the movie _____ yet?

I am _____ in line.

How have you _____ lately?

Where is Ben _____?

108

Left tab labels: next, walk, left, over, done, live, been, shoe, going, house

Review

next
walk
left
over
done
live
been
shoe
going
house

WRITE words to finish the sentences.

| walk | live | house | left | done |

I am _____ with my dinner.

We will _____ at the park.

That is a real, _____ raccoon.

I scraped my _____ knee.

This is my friend's _____.

I _____ on the next block.

The birds have _____ the nest.

next
walk
left
over
done
live
been
shoe
going
house

Review

CONNECT letters in each puzzle to spell three review words. **WRITE** the words on the lines. You will write two words more than once.

x	d	l	a
g	o	i	v
w	n	n	e
m	e	g	f

s	h	o	e
j	o	v	e
z	u	x	r
p	s	e	y

next

walk

left

over

done

live

been

shoe

going

house

_____

_____

_____

_____

w	n	e	x
l	a	q	t
e	b	l	h
f	t	r	k

h	s	h	o
o	c	t	e
u	s	e	i
b	e	e	n

_____

_____

_____

_____

Review

CROSS OUT a word for each clue. WRITE the word that is left over.

It has **on** inside.

It rhymes with **talk**.

It is the opposite of **right**.

It has double **e**.

It begins and ends with the same letter.

It is **evil** backward.

It is the opposite of **under**.

It has **use** inside.

It rhymes with **glue**.

The word that is left is _____.

ask

how

who

then

when

what

them

name

about

would

ask

READ the word. **SAY** it out loud.

I will ask the doctor.

TRACE and **WRITE** the word.

ask

FIND the word. Color the spaces with **ask**.

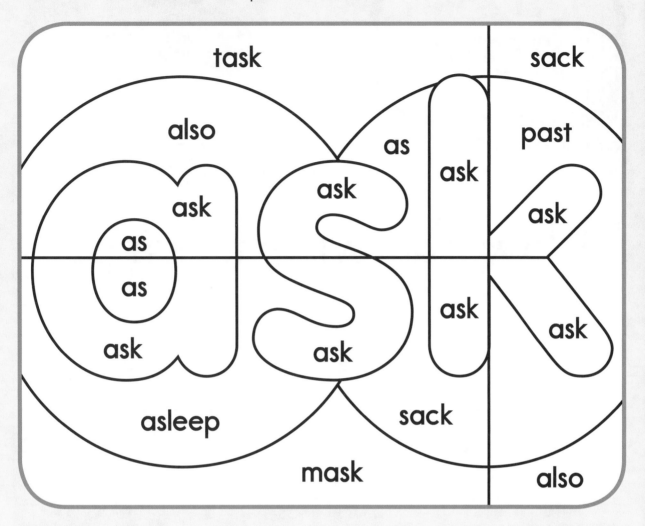

SPELL the word. Circle **ask**.

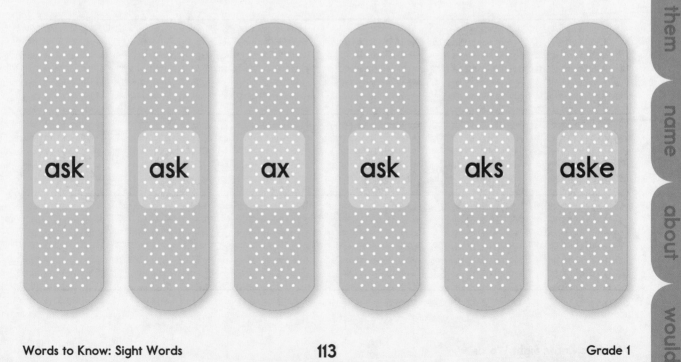

ask   ask   ax   ask   aks   aske

ask
how
who
then
when
what
them
name
about
would

READ the word. **SAY** it out loud.

How far will she jump?

TRACE and **WRITE** the word.

how

how

FIND the word. Draw lines through **how** to see if you won!

who	how	won
wow	how	oh
home	how	hop

how	wow	home
who	how	hop
won	oh	how

SPELL the word. Unscramble the letters to write **how**.

h w o

w h o

_____

o w h

w o h

_____

ask
how
who
then
when
what
them
name
about
would

ask
how
who
then
when
what
them
name
about
would

who

READ the word. SAY it out loud.

Who is hiding?

TRACE and WRITE the word.

COLOR each box with **who**. Match each number to a letter to answer the riddle.

	c	r	m	e	i	a
6	how	was	where	were	what	who
5	when	who	whose	whole	why	hog
4	hold	hole	home	who	horse	hoot
3	who	hood	hoof	zoo	ago	moo
2	two	hero	how	was	who	where
1	were	what	who	when	whose	whole

What is an owl's favorite treat?

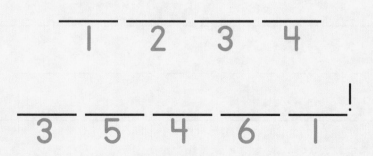

___ ___ ___ ___
 1   2   3   4

___ ___ ___ ___ ___!
 3   5   4   6   1

wask

how

who

then

when

what

them

name

about

would

then

READ the word. **SAY** it out loud.

Tops spin, then they stop.

TRACE and **WRITE** the word.

then

FIND the word in the puzzle. Look → and ↓.

t	h	e	n	t
v	e	t	n	h
k	s	h	q	e
t	h	e	n	n
a	l	n	e	c

SPELL the word. On each xylophone, circle the letters in **then**.

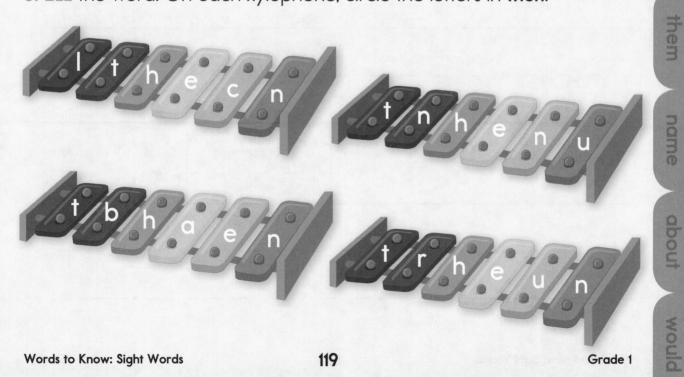

ask
how
who
then
when
what
them
name
about
would

when

READ the word. SAY it out loud.

When will the bubble pop?

TRACE and WRITE the word.

when

when

FIND the word. Circle **when**.

SPELL the word. Write **when** in the puzzle.

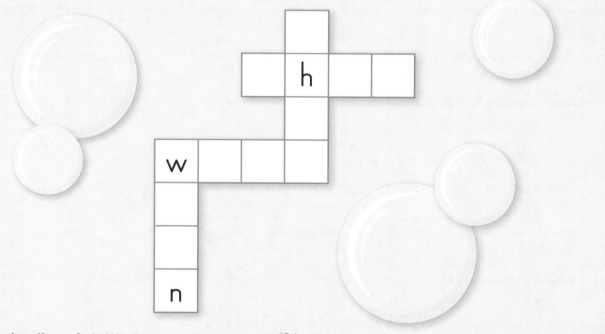

Words to Know: Sight Words 121 Grade 1

what

READ the word. **SAY** it out loud.

What is that creature?

TRACE and **WRITE** the word.

what

what

FIND the word. Color the spaces with **what**.

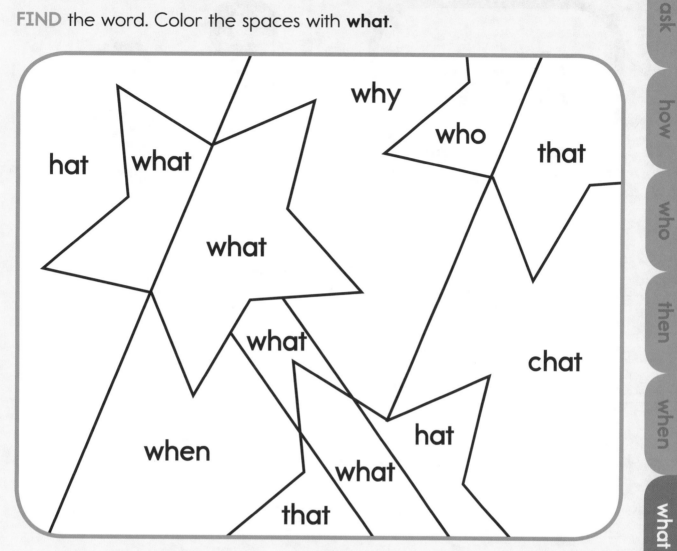

why

who

that

hat

what

what

chat

what

when

hat

what

that

ask

how

who

then

when

what

them

name

about

would

SPELL the word. Write the missing letters.

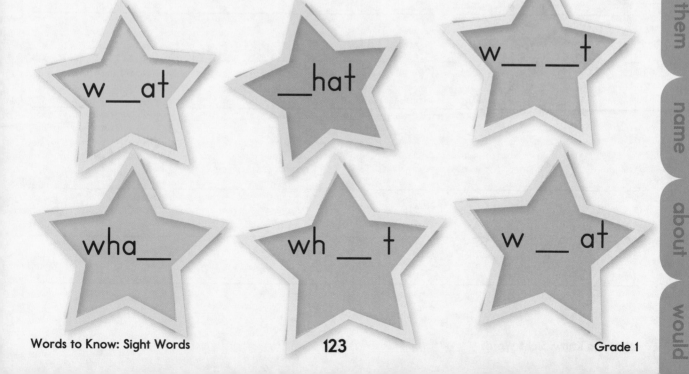

w__at

__hat

w__ __t

wha__

wh __ t

w __ at

them

READ the word. SAY it out loud.

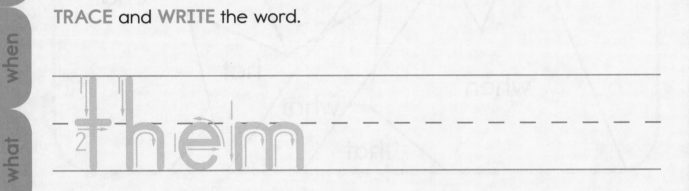

I played with them.

TRACE and WRITE the word.

them

them

FIND the word. Circle **them** in each path.

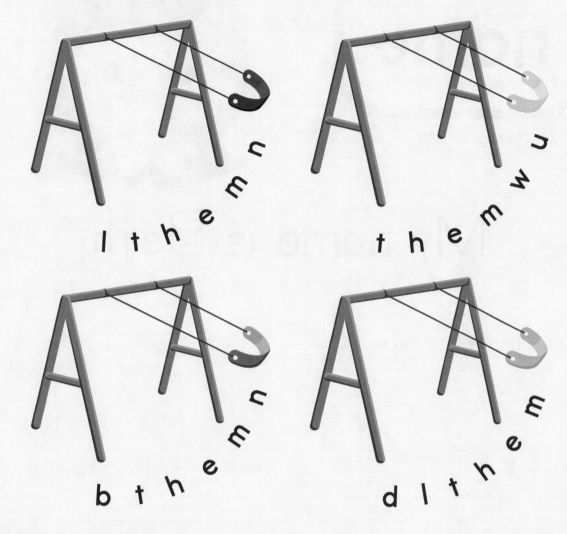

l t h e m n

t h e m w u

b t h e m u

d l t h e m

FIND the word. Circle **them** in each sentence.

I will go down the slide after them.

Take the plates and put them on the table.

Can you see them in the crowd?

ask

how

who

then

when

what

them

name

about

would

ask
how
who
then
when
what
them
name
about
would

READ the word. **SAY** it out loud.

My name is Beth.

TRACE and **WRITE** the word.

FIND the word. Color the pencils with **name**.

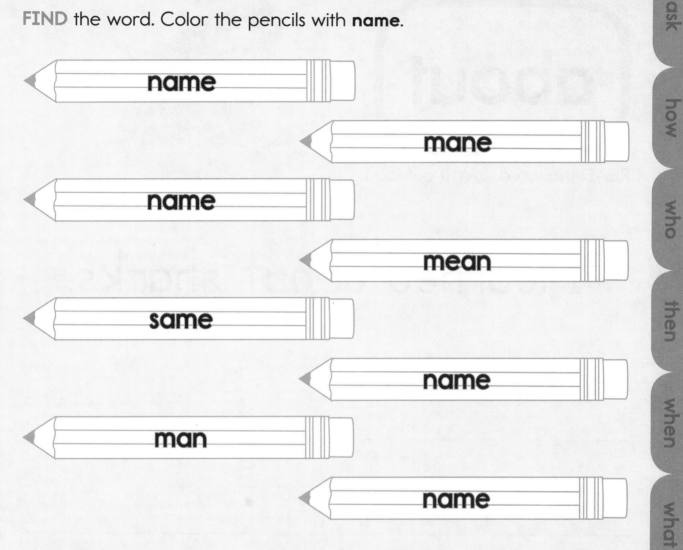

name

mane

name

mean

same

name

man

name

FIND the word. Circle **name**. Draw a box around words that rhyme with **name**.

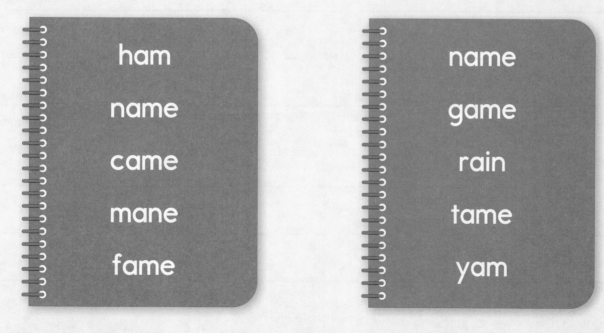

ham

name

came

mane

fame

name

game

rain

tame

yam

ask

how

who

then

when

what

them

name

about

would

READ the word. **SAY** it out loud.

I learned about sharks.

TRACE and **WRITE** the word.

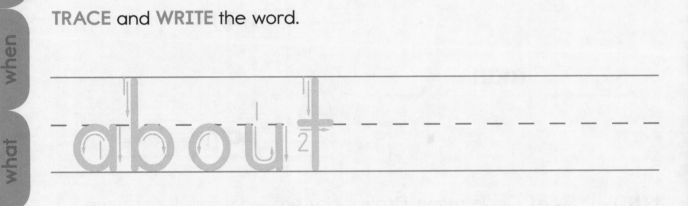

SPELL the word. Complete the word pyramids.

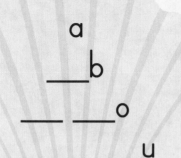

a

___ b

___ ___ o

___ ___ ___ u

___ ___ ___ ___ ___

___

___ ___ ___

___ ___ ___ ___

___ ___ ___ ___ ___

___ ___ ___ ___ ___ ___

FIND the word. Circle **about**.

about   out   about   tuba

boat

about   about   ought

READ the word. **SAY** it out loud.

Would you like a hot dog?

TRACE and **WRITE** the word.

would

would

FIND the word. Color the spaces with **would**.

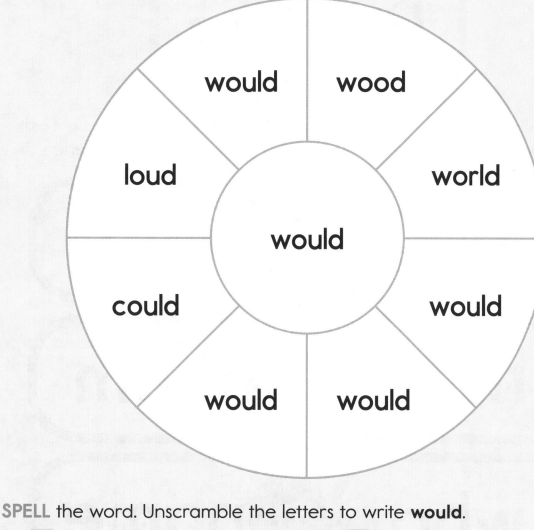

would | wood
loud | world
would *(center)*
could | would
would | would

SPELL the word. Unscramble the letters to write **would**.

uwldo _____

duowl _____

wloud _____

odwul _____

ask

how

who

then

when

what

them

name

about

would

ask
how
who
then
when
what
them
name
about
would

Review

READ the interview on the next page. **FIND** the 10 words. Circle each word you find. Then, write the name of a job to finish the sentence.

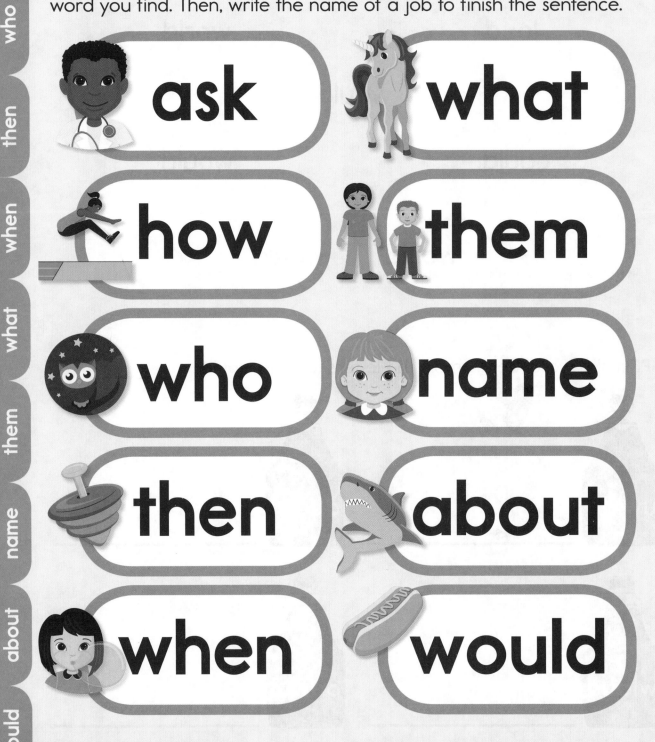

ask

what

how

them

who

name

then

about

when

would

Review

Community Helper Interview

I would like to ask you some questions.

What is your name?

My name is Captain Pat Williams.

When do you work?

I work just about any time, day or night.

Who do you help?

I help people who are in danger from smoke and flames. I keep them safe.

How do you help?

I come in a truck. I use ladders, water, foam, and tools.

What happens then?

When people and buildings are safe, I go back to the station. I wait until I can help again.

Captain Williams is a _____.

ask
how
who
then
when
what
them
name
about
would

ask
how
who
then
when
what
them
name
about
would

Review

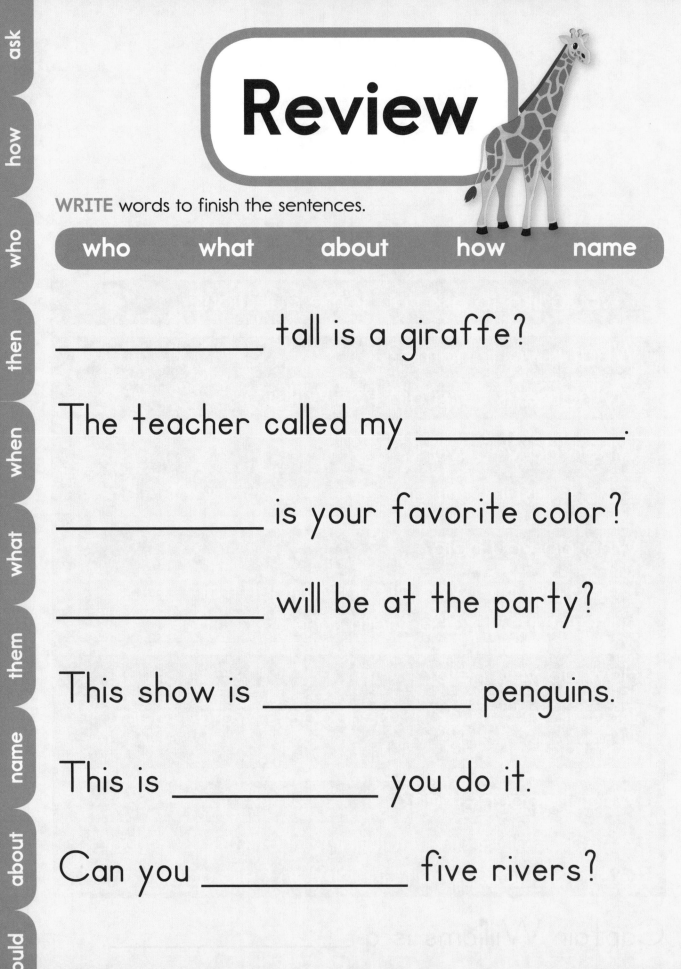

WRITE words to finish the sentences.

who	what	about	how	name

_____ tall is a giraffe?

The teacher called my _____.

_____ is your favorite color?

_____ will be at the party?

This show is _____ penguins.

This is _____ you do it.

Can you _____ five rivers?

Review

ask

how

who

then

when

what

them

name

about

would

WRITE words to finish the sentences.

| ask | them | then | when | would |

_____ do lions sleep and hunt?

I have a question to _____.

They want me to go with _____.

What game _____ you like?

We played, and _____ we ate.

We need to _____ for help.

How _____ you like your eggs?

Review

WRITE words. Use the code to help you.

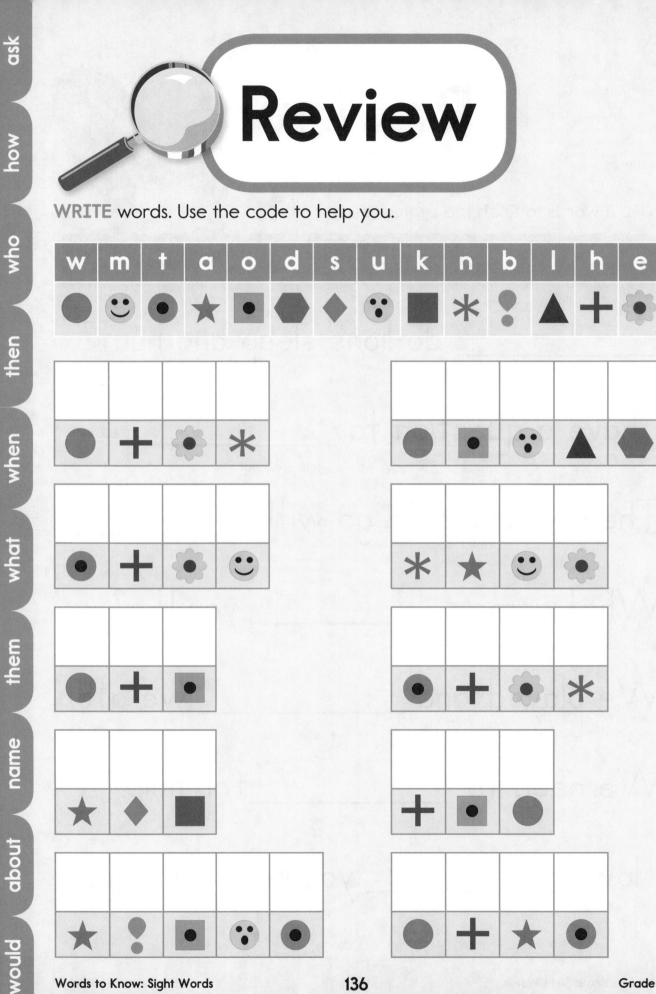

| w | m | t | a | o | d | s | u | k | n | b | l | h | e |

when

would

them

name

who

then

ask

how

about

what

Review

WRITE letters to complete the words. Use the color code to finish the joke.

ask	who	when	them	about
how	then	what	name	would

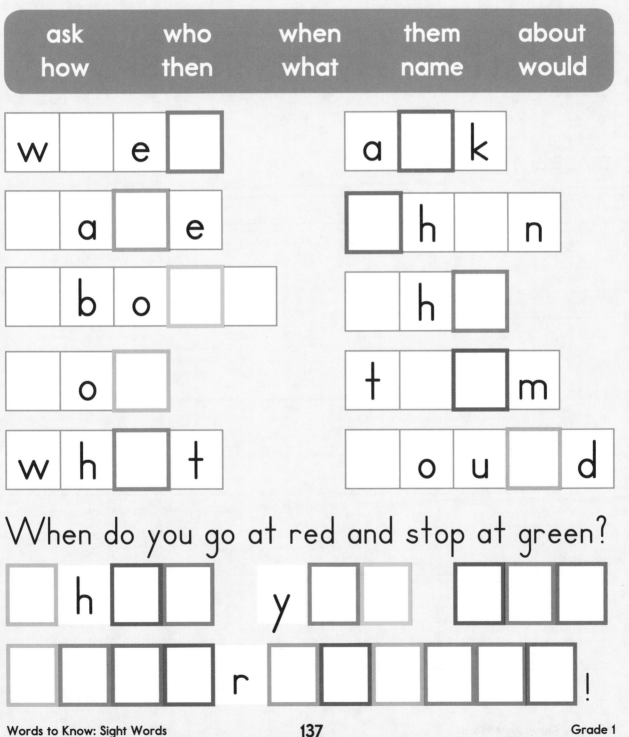

When do you go at red and stop at green?

fly

READ the word. **SAY** it out loud.

Kites fly in the sky.

TRACE and **WRITE** the word.

f l y

f l y

FIND the word in the puzzle. Look ➡ and ⬇.

s	q	f	o	v
f	l	y	f	u
s	f	m	l	f
g	l	f	y	l
b	y	q	p	y

SPELL the word. On each kite tail, circle the letters in **fly**.

Kite tail letters:
1. f, b / t, l / p, y
2. t, f / l, i / y, j
3. f, h / t, l / g, y
4. l, f / i, l / y, q

Words to Know: Sight Words

139

Grade 1

fish each grow small some take water under round

fly

fly
fish
each
grow
small
some
take
water
under
round

fish

READ the word. SAY it out loud.

Fish use gills to breathe.

TRACE and WRITE the word.

COUNT fish. Write the number on the fish food.

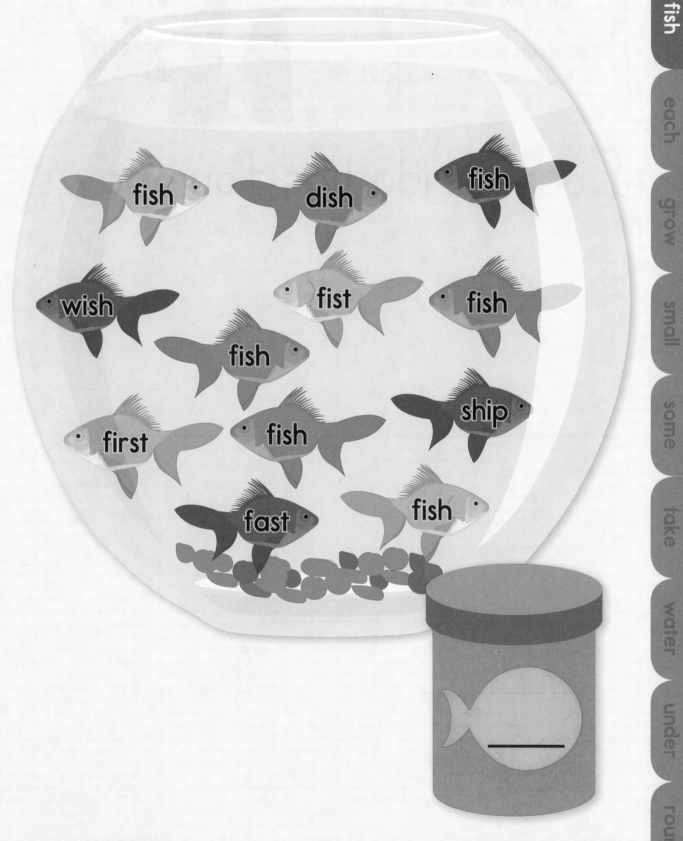

READ the word. **SAY** it out loud.

Each panda has four paws.

TRACE and **WRITE** the word.

each

each

FIND the word. Color the spaces with **each**.

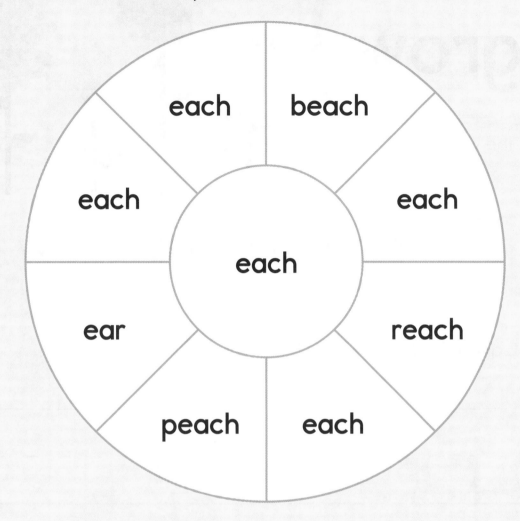

SPELL the word. Match the letters in **each**.

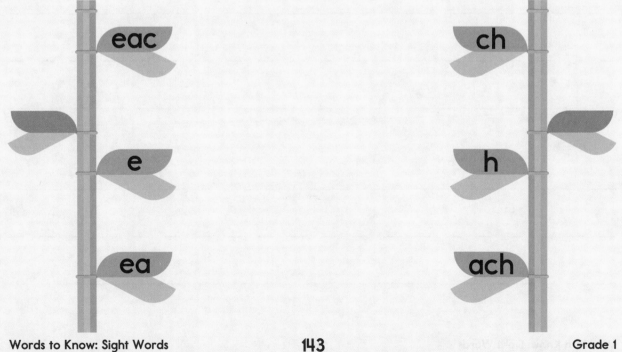

fly fish each grow small some take water under round

grow

READ the word. **SAY** it out loud.

The flowers will grow.

TRACE and **WRITE** the word.

grow

grow

FIND the word. Circle **grow**.

SPELL the word. On each flower, circle the letters in **grow**.

fly
fish
each
grow
small
some
take
water
under
round

fly
fish
each
grow
small
some
take
water
under
round

small

READ the word. **SAY** it out loud.

The orange ball is small.

TRACE and **WRITE** the word.

FIND the word. Draw lines through **small** to see if you won!

small	all	mall
smart	small	smile
malls	stall	small

all	mall	smart
smile	stall	malls
small	small	small

WRITE small beside the smaller object in each pair.

_____   _____

_____   _____

_____   _____

fly
fish
each
grow
small
some
take
water
under
round

fly
fish
each
grow
small
some
take
water
under
round

some

READ the word. SAY it out loud.

I want **some** ice cream.

TRACE and WRITE the word.

some

some

FIND the word. Color the spaces with **some**.

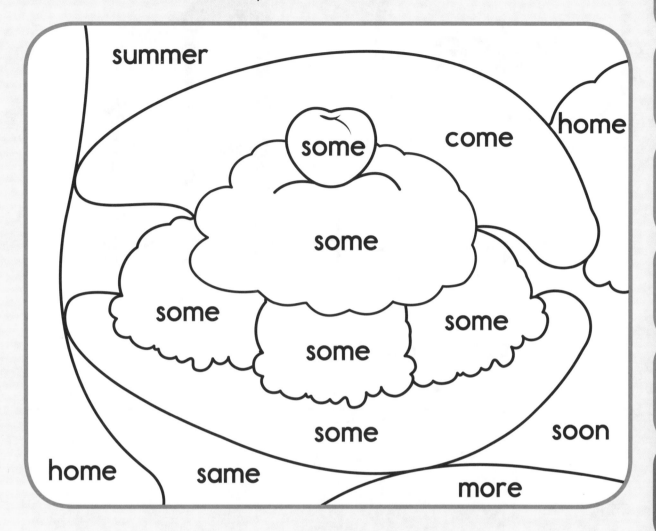

SPELL the word. On each scoop, circle the letters in **some**.

fly   fish   each   grow   small   some   take   water   under   round

fly
fish
each
grow
small
some
take
water
under
round

take

READ the word. **SAY** it out loud.

Take me to the park.

TRACE and **WRITE** the word.

FIND the word. Circle **take**. Draw a box around words that rhyme with **take**.

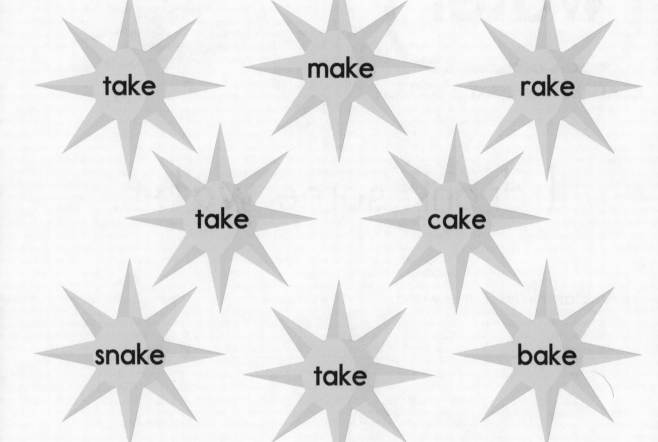

take

make

rake

take

cake

snake

take

bake

SPELL the word. In each puzzle, connect letters to spell **take**.

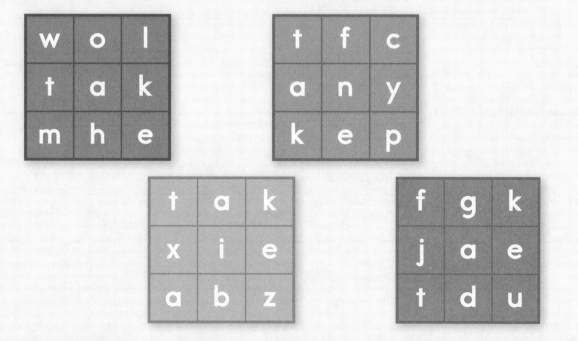

w	o	l
t	a	k
m	h	e

t	f	c
a	n	y
k	e	p

t	a	k
x	i	e
a	b	z

f	g	k
j	a	e
t	d	u

fly fish each grow small some take water under round

fly
fish
each
grow
small
some
take
water
under
round

READ the word. **SAY** it out loud.

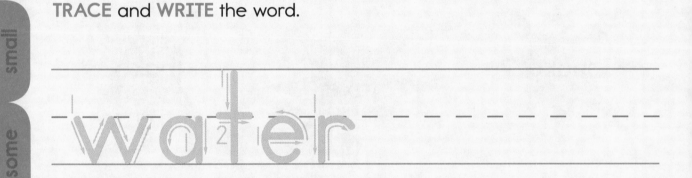

I drank some water.

TRACE and **WRITE** the word.

water

water

COLOR each box with **water**. Match each number to a letter to answer the riddle.

fly
fish
each
grow
small
some
take
water
under
round

	l	t	i	t	e
5	waiter	what	later	wader	water
4	water	raw	treat	wait	wheat
3	waffle	water	wake	wave	wagon
2	want	warn	water	watch	watery
1	eater	waiter	what	water	later

What do you get when you throw books into the ocean?

A ___ ___ ___ ___ ___ wave!
   1   2   3   4   5

fly

fish

each

grow

small

some

take

water

under

round

under

READ the word. **SAY** it out loud.

My bear is under the table.

TRACE and **WRITE** the word.

FIND the word. Circle **under** in each sentence. Then, draw a line to the matching picture.

My ball is under the umbrella.

Is my ball under the chair?

My ball must be under the rug!

SPELL the word. Unscramble the letters to write **under**.

fly

fish

each

grow

small

some

take

water

under

round

fly fish each grow small some take water under round

round

READ the word. **SAY** it out loud.

The cookie is round.

TRACE and **WRITE** the word.

round

round

_____

_ _ _ _ _ _ _ _ _ _

_____

SPELL the word. Connect the letters in **round**.

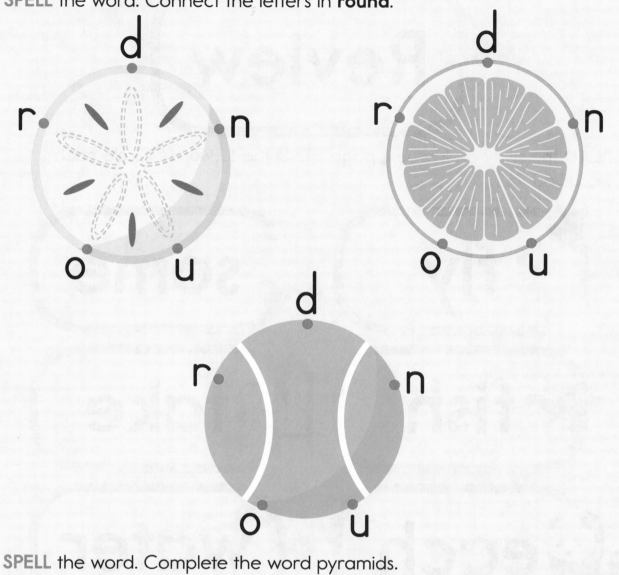

SPELL the word. Complete the word pyramids.

r

___ o

___ ___ u

___ o ___ n

___ ___ u ___ d

___

___ ___ ___

___ ___ ___ ___

___ ___ ___ ___ ___

Review

READ the story on the next page. FIND the 10 words. Circle each word you find.

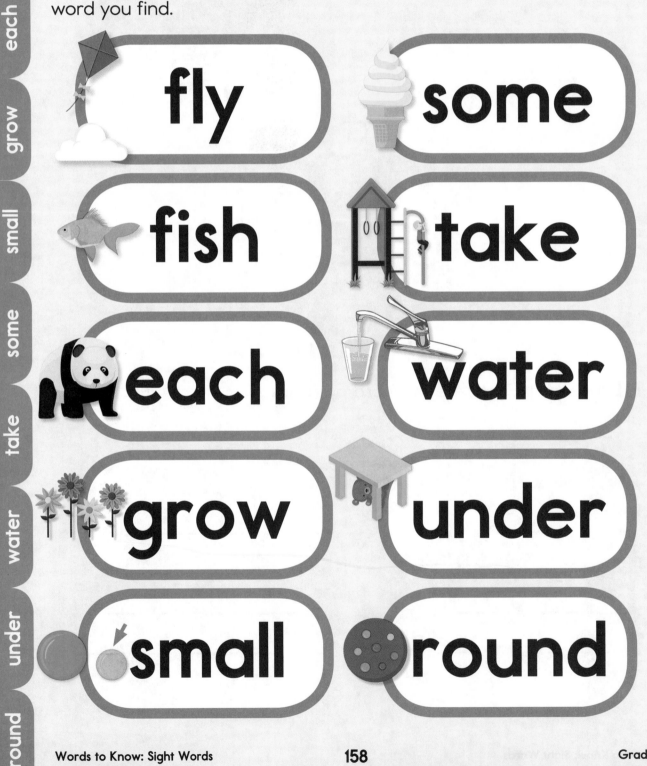

fly

some

fish

take

each

water

grow

under

small

round

Review

Wishing for Fish

Sadie sat on the dock. She tried to see under the water. Were some fish down there?

Sadie saw a small ripple on the water. Was that a fish? No, it was only a fly.

Then, Sadie saw some round rings on the water. She watched each circle grow bigger and bigger. Was that a fish? She heard her brother laugh. When she looked up, she saw him tossing rocks into the water. "Stop it!" she said. "Come help me look for a fish."

Bryce sat by Sadie. They were both quiet. Suddenly, a seagull swooped down. The kids watched the bird take a floppy thing from the water. "I know what that was!" said Sadie. "I saw a fish!"

Review

WRITE words to finish the sentences.

| grow | take | under | fish | each |

_____ a tomato from my garden.

I _____ taller every year.

We like to _____ at the lake.

Boats go _____ the bridge.

Give a paper to _____ student.

Some _____ have colorful scales.

What costs _____ five dollars?

fly

fish

each

grow

small

some

take

water

under

round

Review 1¢

WRITE words to finish the sentences.

fly   small   some   water   round

A penny has a _____ shape.

All plants need _____.

I ordered a _____ popcorn.

This chore will take _____ time.

Bats are mammals that can _____.

Please _____ up all the crayons.

_____ the garden each week.

fly fish each grow small some take water under round

fly
fish
each
grow
small
some
take
water
under
round

Review

WRITE a word in the puzzle to complete each sentence.

| fly | each | small | take | under |
| fish | grow | some | water | round |

ACROSS

2. We will ___ on a plane.

4. I keep ___ things in my pocket.

5. The principal came to ___ class.

6. ___ filled the tub.

9. Would you like ___ soup?

DOWN

1. I got ___ the covers.

2. Dad cooked ___ on the grill.

3. What will I be when I ___ up?

7. Let's ___ a bike ride.

8. Wheels are ___.

Review

CROSS OUT a word for each clue. WRITE the word that is left over.

It rhymes with **wall**.

It is **teach** without **t**.

It can name one animal or many animals.

It spells the long **i** sound with **y**.

It has **ate** inside.

It begins with the short **u** sound.

It rhymes with **bake**.

It is **growl** without **l**.

It has **me** inside.

The word that is left is _____ .

open
from
give
thank
happy
pretty
table
present
friend

wish

READ the word. **SAY** it out loud.

I wish for a new toy.

TRACE and **WRITE** the word.

FIND the word in the puzzle. Look → and ↓.

n	x	g	w	o
w	g	w	i	o
i	w	i	s	h
s	q	s	h	f
h	k	h	g	u

WRITE wish in each sentence. Draw what you wish for.

I _____ for [_____] .

I _____ for [_____] .

Words to Know: Sight Words

Grade 1

wish

open

from

give

thank

happy

pretty

table

present

friend

wish

open

from

give

thank

happy

pretty

table

present

friend

READ the word. **SAY** it out loud.

Butterfy wings can open.

TRACE and **WRITE** the word.

open

FIND the word. Draw lines through **open** to see if you won!

pen	one	nope
poem	pan	close
open	open	open

open	nope	poem
open	one	pen
open	pan	close

WRITE open beside the object that is open in each pair.

_____   _____

_____   _____

_____

wish
open
from
give
thank
happy
pretty
table
present
friend

wish

open

from

give

thank

happy

pretty

table

present

friend

from

READ the word. SAY it out loud.

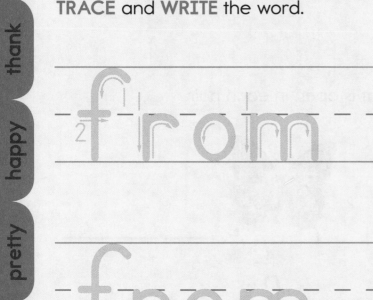

Aliens came from space.

TRACE and WRITE the word.

from

from

FIND the word. Circle **from**.

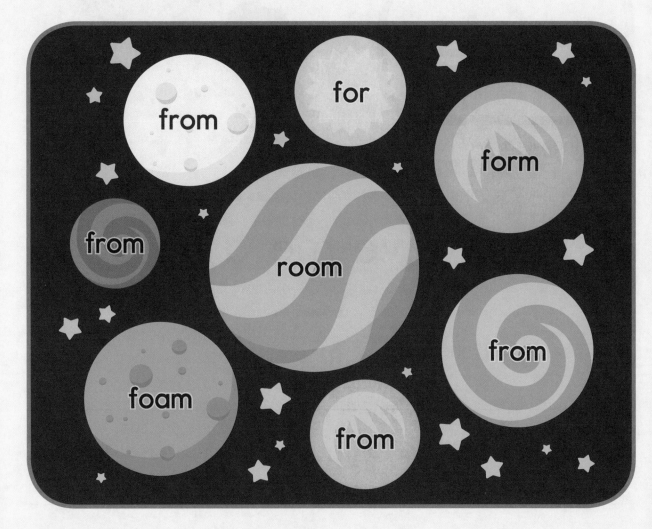

FIND the word. Circle **from** in each comet tail.

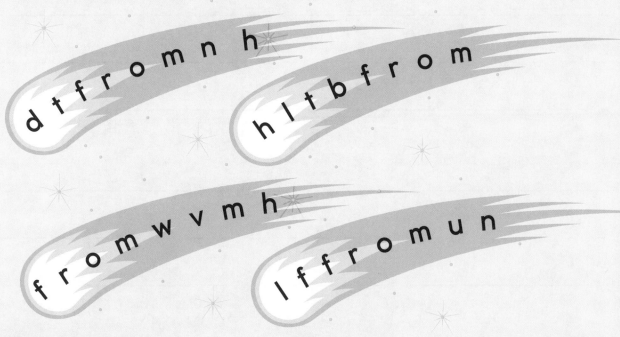

d t f r o m n h

h l t b f r o m

f r o m w v m h

l f f r o m u n

give

READ the word. **SAY** it out loud.

Please give me a balloon.

TRACE and **WRITE** the word.

give

give

FIND the word. Color the balloons with **give**.

give

five

give

live

dive

give

give

hive

SPELL the word. Unscramble the letters to write **give**.

g i e v

i e g v

v i e g

e g i v

_____

_____

_____

_____

wish
open
from
give
thank
happy
pretty
table
present
friend

thank

READ the word. **SAY** it out loud.

Thank farmers for food.

TRACE and **WRITE** the word.

thank

thank

FIND the word. Color the spaces with **thank**.

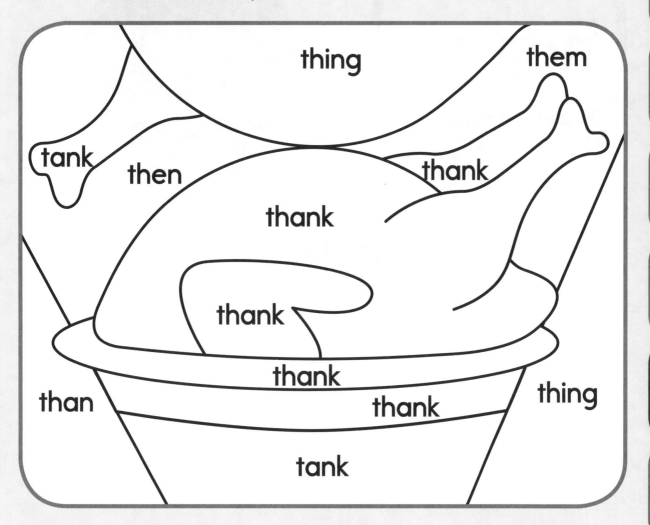

SPELL the word. Match the letters in **thank**.

wish
open
from
give
thank
happy
pretty
table
present
friend

happy

READ the word. **SAY** it out loud.

I feel **happy**!

TRACE and **WRITE** the word.

FIND the word. Color the spaces with **happy**.

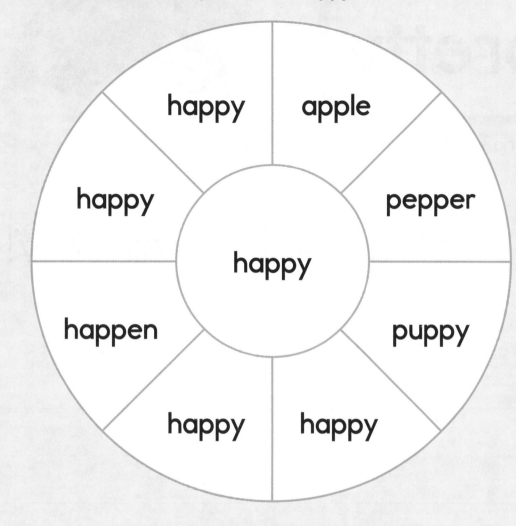

SPELL the word. Write the missing letters. Use the code.

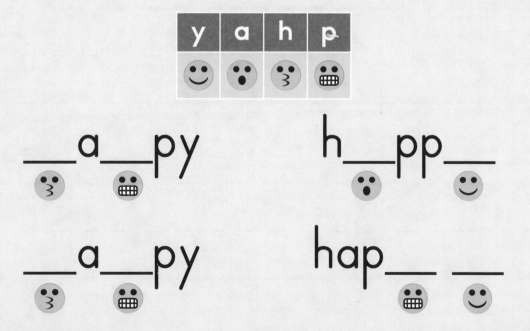

wish
open
from
give
thank
happy
pretty
table
present
friend

pretty

READ the word. **SAY** it out loud.

What a pretty rainbow!

TRACE and **WRITE** the word.

pretty

pretty

FIND the word. Circle **pretty**.

pretty pretty kitty

better pretty

little pretty patty

SPELL the word. In each arc, circle the letters in **pretty**.

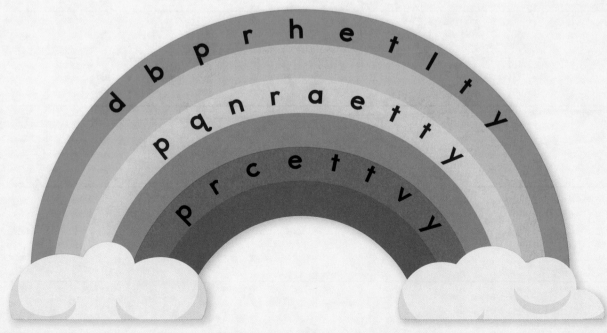

d b p r h e t l t y

p q n r a e t t y

p r c e t t v y

wish open from give thank happy pretty table present friend

wish open from give thank happy pretty table present friend

table

READ the word. SAY it out loud.

I set the table.

TRACE and WRITE the word.

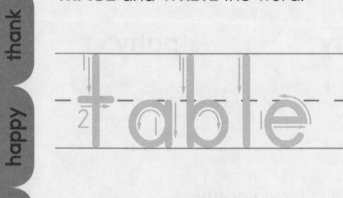

FIND the word. Color the plates with **table**.

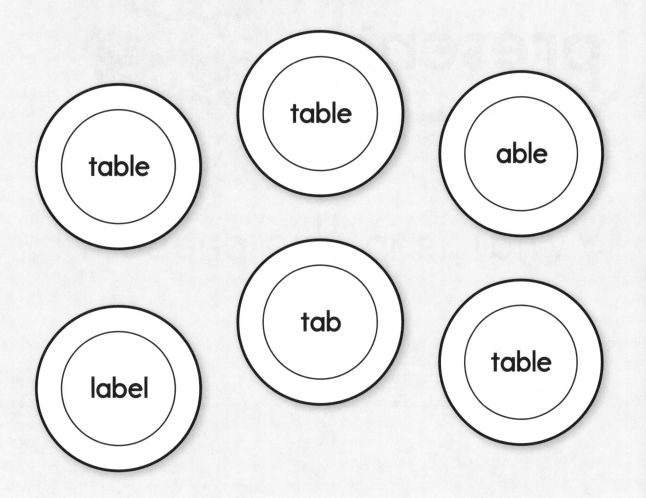

SPELL the word. Circle **table**.

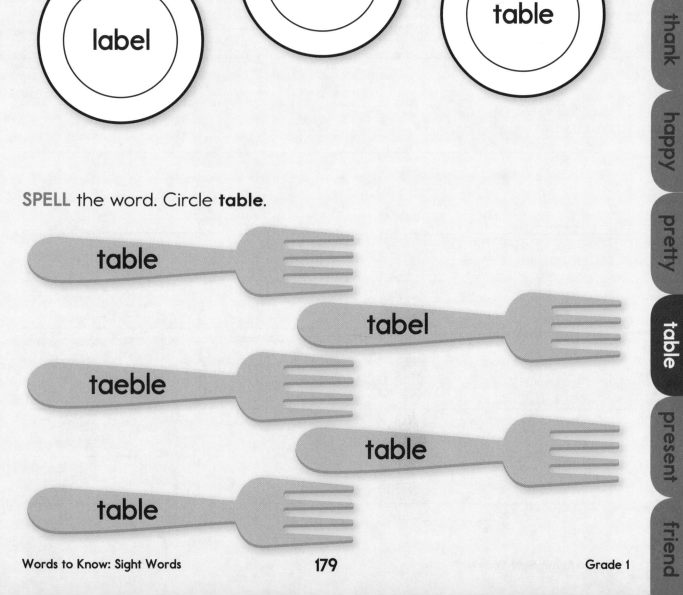

wish open from give thank happy pretty table present friend

wish
open
from
give
thank
happy
pretty
table
present
friend

present

READ the word. SAY it out loud.

What is in this present?

TRACE and WRITE the word.

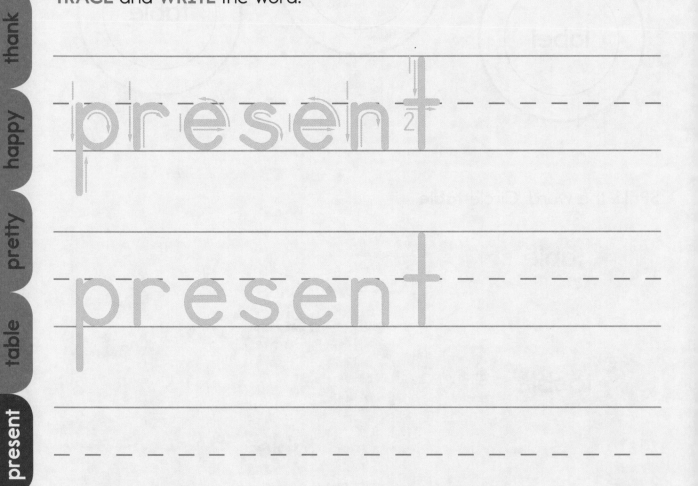

present

present

SPELL the word. Complete the word pyramids.

p

___r

___ ___e

___ r ___s

p ___ e ___ e

___ ___ ___ s ___ n

p ___ ___ ___ ___ ___ t

___

___ ___

___ ___ ___ ___

___ ___ ___ ___ ___

___ ___ ___ ___ ___ ___

___ ___ ___ ___ ___ ___ ___

READ the word. **SAY** it out loud.

This is my friend.

TRACE and **WRITE** the word.

friend

SPELL the word. Circle **friend**.

SPELL the word. Write **friend** in the puzzle.

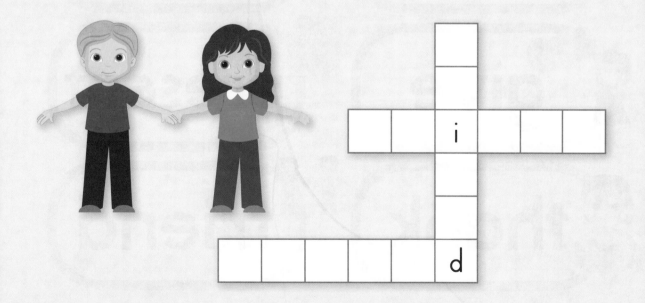

Words to Know: Sight Words

183

Grade 1

Review

READ the list on the next page. FIND the 10 words. Circle each word you find.

wish

happy

open

pretty

from

table

give

present

thank

friend

Review

Things to Do at My Birthday Party

- ☐ Put pretty decorations on the table.

- ☐ Say hello to each friend.

- ☐ Play fun games!

- ☐ Sing Happy Birthday. Blow out the candles and make a wish.

- ☐ Open presents. Ask who each present is from. Thank the giver.

- ☐ Give a treat to each friend.

wish   open   from   give   thank   happy   pretty   table   present   friend

Review

WRITE words to finish the sentences.

thank	present	wish	pretty	table

You have a _____ cat.

All 20 students are _____.

I _____ I could see you.

We do crafts at the _____.

_____ you for helping me!

This is a _____ for you.

That is a _____ tall tree!

Review

wish
open
from
give
thank
happy
pretty
table
present
friend

Reggie
Chloe

WRITE words to finish the sentences.

happy	give	from	friend	open

The letter is _____ Reggie.

Reggie is my _____.

His family is _____ Florida.

I cannot wait to _____ the letter.

I am _____ to hear from him!

I will _____ him a picture I made.

I hope it will make him _____.

wish
open
from
give
thank
happy
pretty
table
present
friend

Review

MATCH the words. Use the codes to complete the jokes.

1. friend   give   **e**
2. give   open   **e**
3. thank   present   **c**
4. present   friend   **f**
5. open   thank   **n**

What runs around the yard while standing still? A ___ ___ ___ ___ ___ !
① ② ③ ④ ⑤

1. wish   table   **o**
2. happy   pretty   **c**
3. table   wish   **c**
4. pretty   from   **k**
5. from   happy   **l**

What has a face and hands, but no arms and legs? A ___ ___ ___ ___ ___ !
① ② ③ ④ ⑤

Review

COLOR the words that are spelled correctly. **WRITE** letters to complete the words.

t__b__e   tha__ __

__ish   ha__ __y

o__e__   pr__tt__

__riend   giv__

fr__m   pr__s__nt

just

ride

slow

more

once

could

money

every

leave

READ the word. **SAY** it out loud.

Stop at the sign.

TRACE and **WRITE** the word.

s top

stop

FIND the word. Color the cars with **stop**.

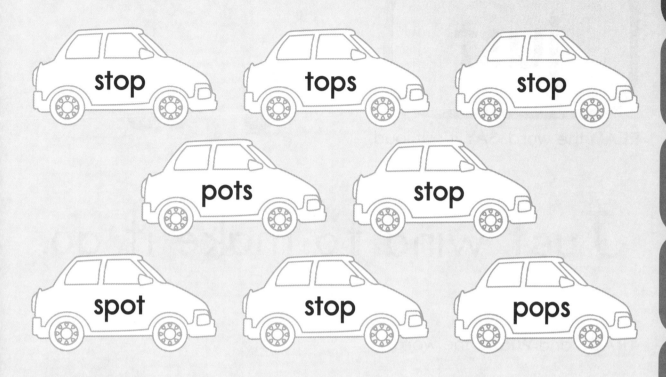

SPELL the word. Circle **stop**.

stop

just

ride

slow

more

once

could

money

every

leave

stop

just

ride

slow

more

once

could

money

every

leave

just

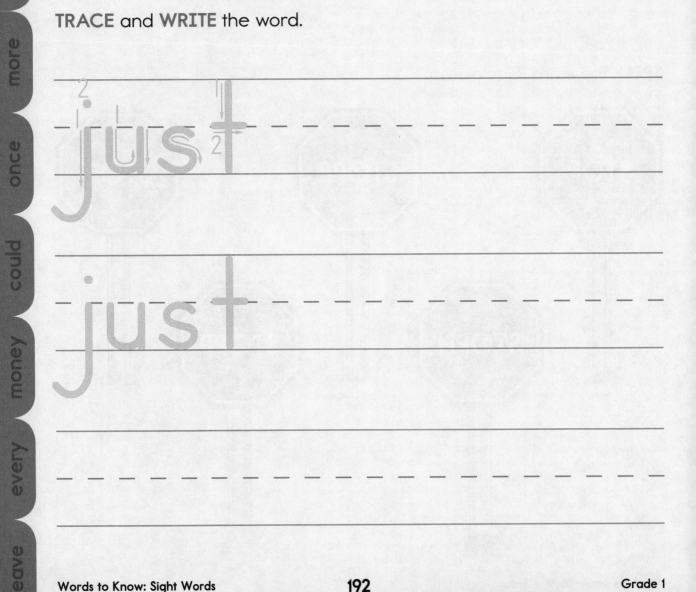

READ the word. **SAY** it out loud.

Just wind to make it go.

TRACE and **WRITE** the word.

just

just

COUNT just and write the number. **COUNT** the words that rhyme with **just** and write the number.

just	Rhymes with just
_____	_____

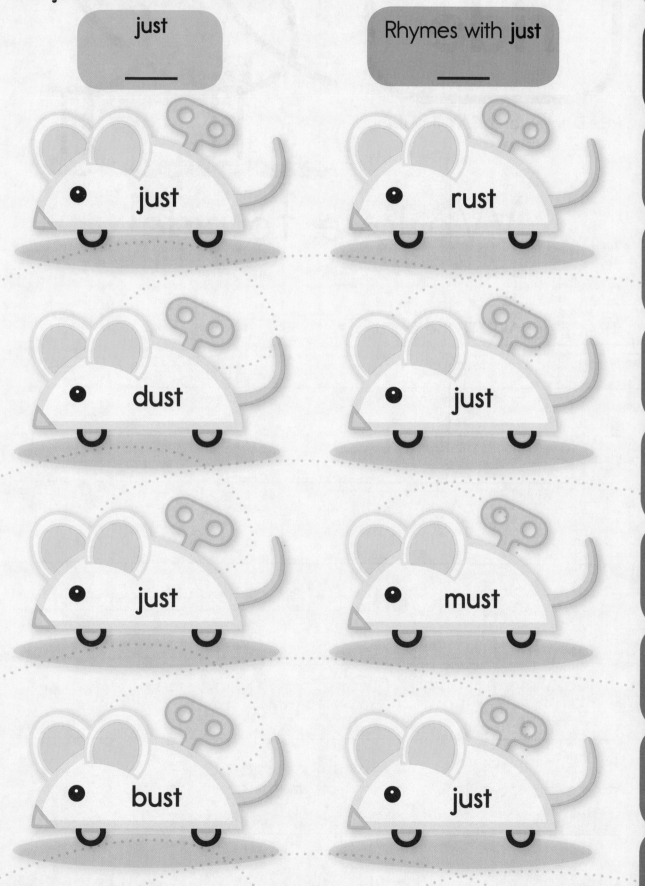

just

rust

dust

just

just

must

bust

just

stop
just
ride
slow
more
once
could
money
every
leave

stop
just
ride
slow
more
once
could
money
every
leave

ride

READ the word. SAY it out loud.

We love to ride!

TRACE and WRITE the word.

ride

ride

FIND the word in the puzzle. Look → and ↓.

e	r	i	d	e
r	i	f	k	q
i	r	i	d	e
d	k	n	i	f
e	r	i	d	e

SPELL the word on each car. Write the missing letters.

_ _id   r _ _d   _ i _ e   r _ _ e

stop

just

ride

slow

more

once

could

money

every

leave

stop
just
ride
slow
more
once
could
money
every
leave

READ the word. **SAY** it out loud.

Snails are slow.

TRACE and **WRITE** the word.

slow

FIND the word. Color the spaces with **slow**.

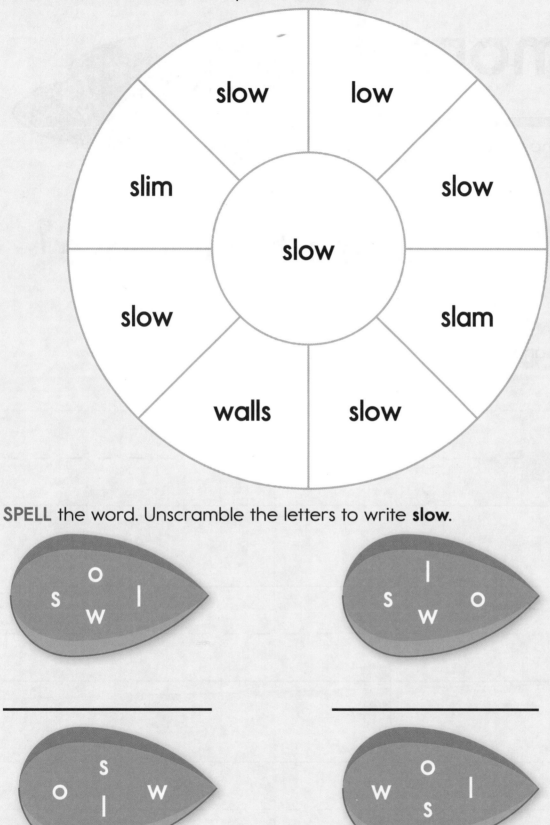

SPELL the word. Unscramble the letters to write **slow**.

stop

just

ride

slow

more

once

could

money

every

leave

Words to Know: Sight Words   197   Grade 1

stop · just · ride · slow · more · once · could · money · every · leave

more

READ the word. **SAY** it out loud.

May I please have more?

TRACE and **WRITE** the word.

more

more

FIND the word. Color the spaces with **more**.

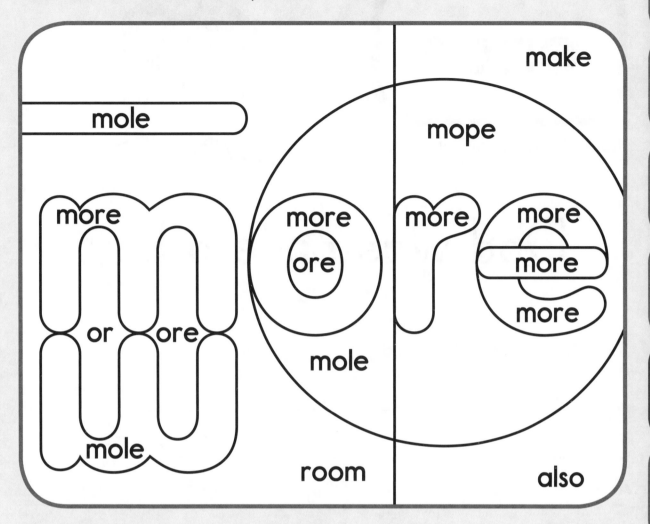

SPELL the word. Complete the word pyramids.

stop
just
ride
slow
more
once
could
money
every
leave

stop

just

ride

slow

more

once

could

money

every

leave

READ the word. **SAY** it out loud.

Dad was once a boy.

TRACE and **WRITE** the word.

once

once

FIND the word. Draw lines through **once** to see if you won!

one	only	once
inch	cone	once
onto	cent	once

onto	inch	cent
once	once	once
cone	one	only

FIND the word. Circle **once** in each title.

Once Upon a Time

She Once Sailed the Sea

Once and Done

He Was Once a King

Once I Can Fly

stop
just
ride
slow
more
once
could
money
every
leave

stop

just

ride

slow

more

once

could

money

every

leave

could

READ the word. **SAY** it out loud.

Could we take a trip?

TRACE and **WRITE** the word.

could

could

FIND the word. Color the spaces with **could**.

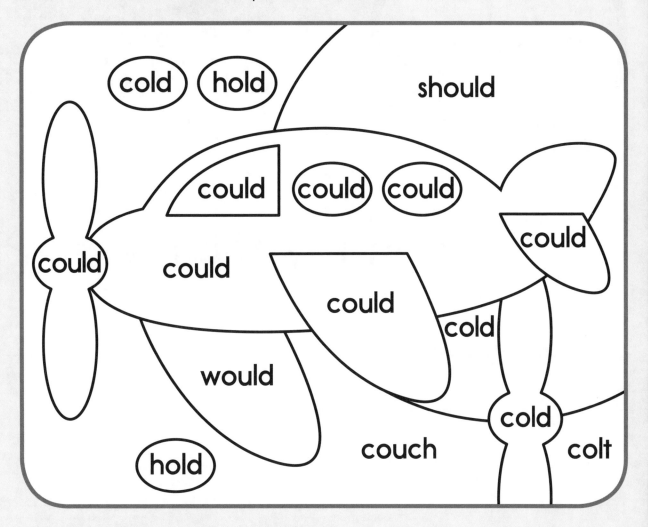

SPELL the word. Connect the letters in **could**.

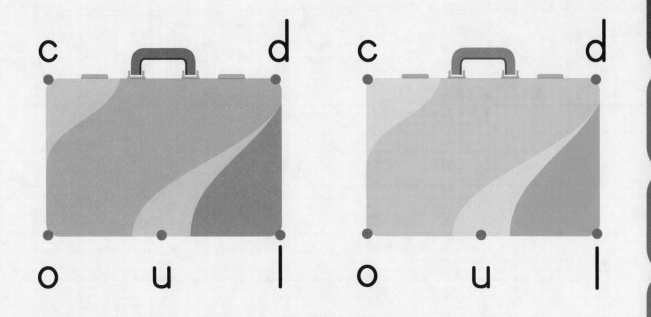

stop
just
ride
slow
more
once
could
money
every
leave

READ the word. **SAY** it out loud.

I saved my money.

TRACE and **WRITE** the word.

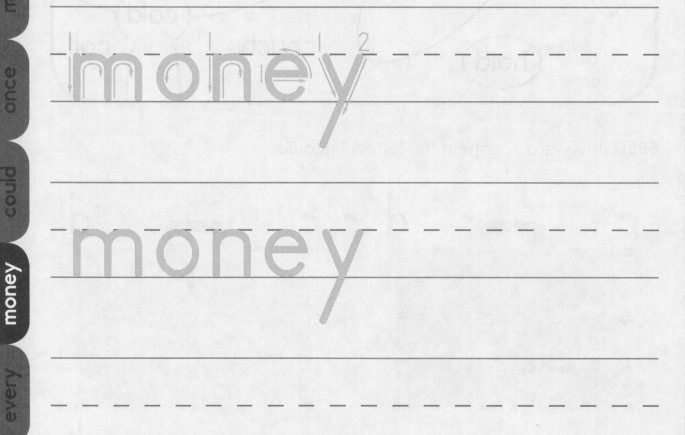

money

money

FIND the word. Color the tags with **money**.

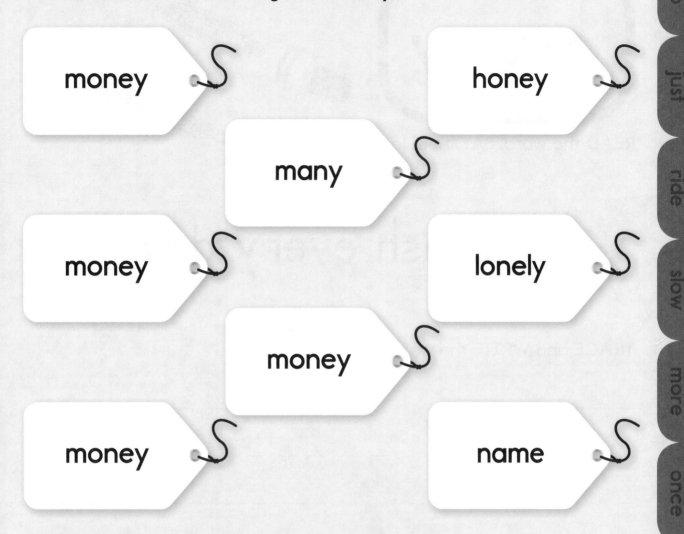

money

honey

many

money

lonely

money

money

name

SPELL the word. Unscramble the letters to write **money**.

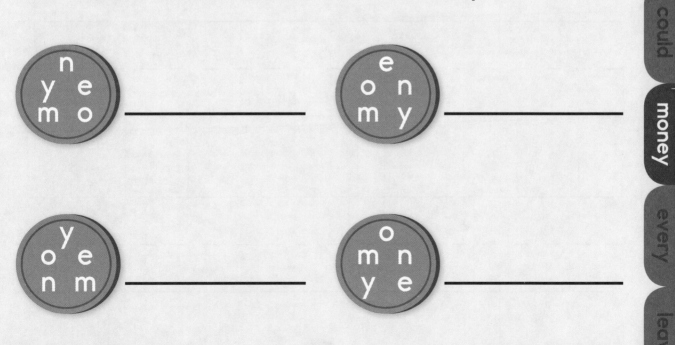

n y e m o _____

e o n m y _____

y o e n m _____

o m n y e _____

stop just ride slow more once could money every leave

stop

just

ride

slow

more

once

could

money

every

leave

every

READ the word. **SAY** it out loud.

I brush **every** day.

TRACE and **WRITE** the word.

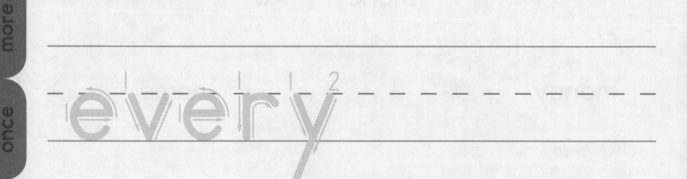

every

every

FIND the word. Circle **every** in each row.

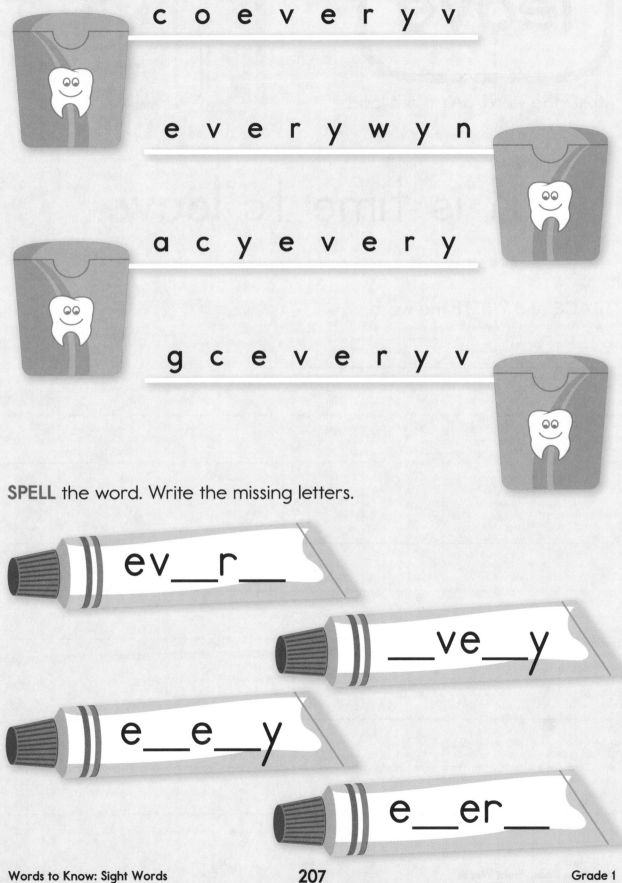

c o **e v e r y** v

e v e r y w y n

a c y **e v e r y**

g c **e v e r y** v

SPELL the word. Write the missing letters.

ev__r__

__ve__y

e__e__y

e__er__

stop
just
ride
slow
more
once
could
money
every
leave

READ the word. **SAY** it out loud.

It is time to leave.

TRACE and **WRITE** the word.

leave

leave

FIND the word. Circle **leave**.

SPELL the word. Write **leave** in the puzzle.

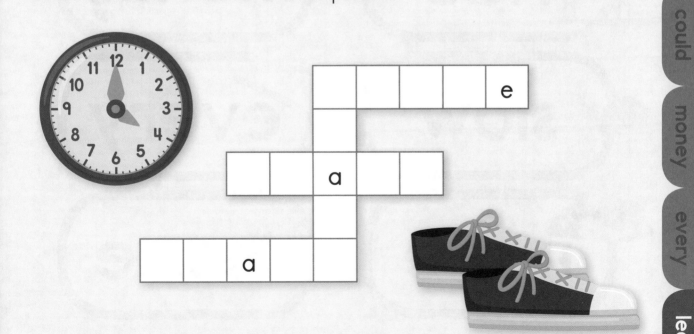

stop
just
ride
slow
more
once
could
money
every
leave

stop
just
ride
slow
more
once
could
money
every
leave

Review

READ the craft idea on the next page. FIND the 10 words. Circle each word you find.

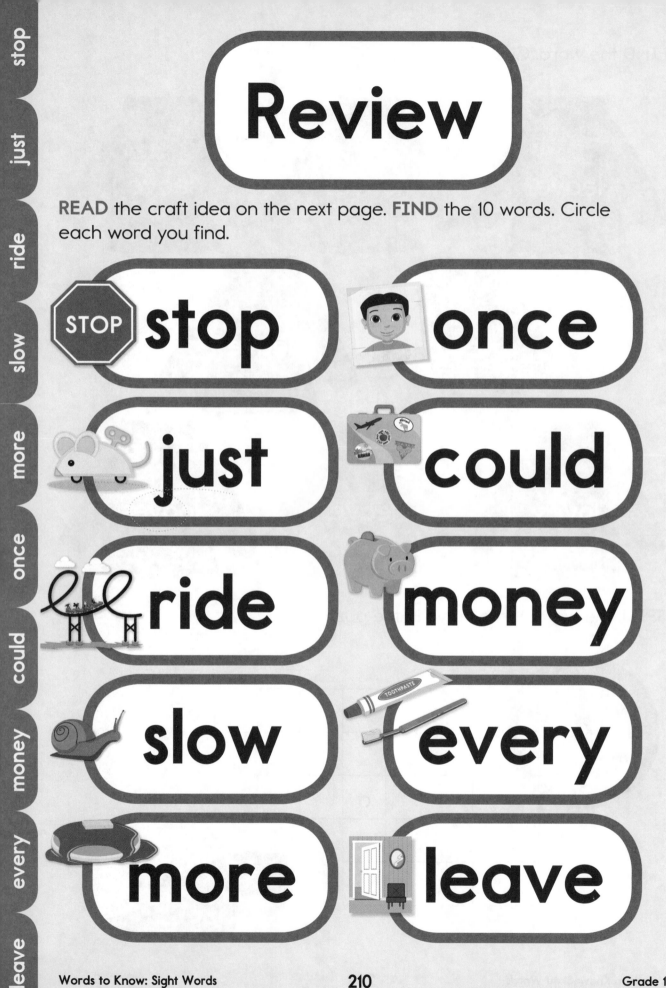

STOP stop

once

just

could

ride

money

slow

every

more

leave

Review

Piggy Bank Craft

Make a piggy bank! Just find an empty plastic bottle, colored paper, scissors, glue, four bottle lids, a pipe cleaner, and a knife.

Ask an adult to use the knife to cut a slit in the bottle. Stop when it is big enough for a quarter. Once that is done, cut ears, eyes, and a nose from paper. Slow down and think of more ideas. You could make a surfboard for your pig to ride or glasses for it to wear. Glue the paper on the bottle. Leave space so you can glue on the lids to make feet. Add a pipe cleaner tail, too.

Do not forget to put money in your bank every day!

stop
just
ride
slow
more
once
could
money
every
leave

Review

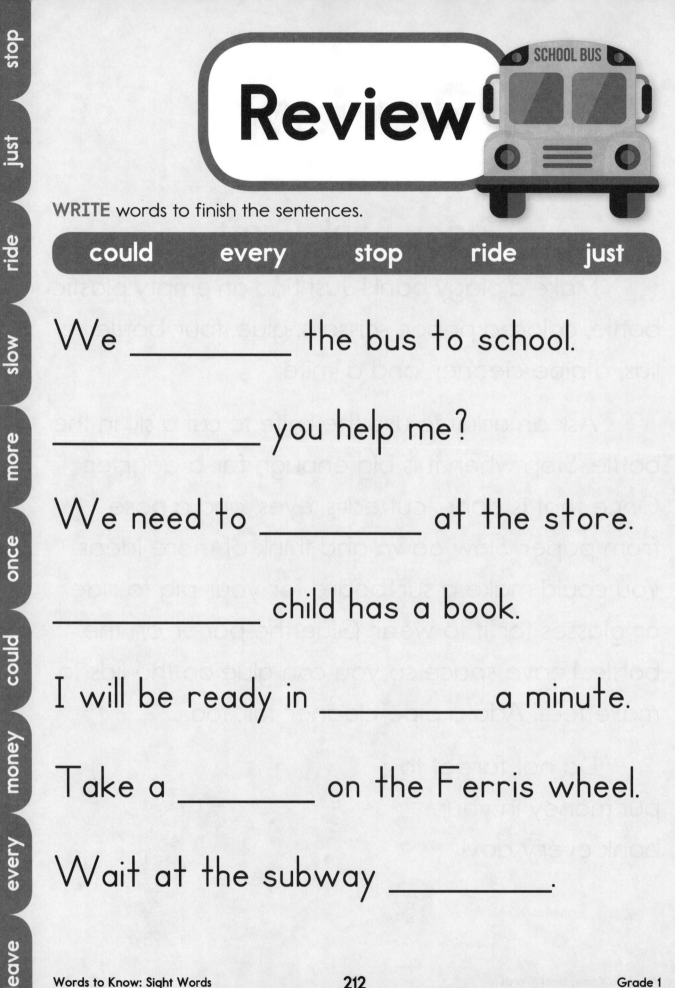

WRITE words to finish the sentences.

could	every	stop	ride	just

We _____ the bus to school.

_____ you help me?

We need to _____ at the store.

_____ child has a book.

I will be ready in _____ a minute.

Take a _____ on the Ferris wheel.

Wait at the subway _____.

Review

stop
just
ride
slow
more
once
could
money
every
leave

WRITE words to finish the sentences.

slow	more	once	money	leave

Do we have _____ cheese?

I have enough _____.

Call me _____ you get home.

_____ down or you will fall!

Did Jamie _____ the party?

I have been there _____ before.

_____ the dirty dishes for us.

stop
just
ride
slow
more
once
could
money
every
leave

Review

FIND the words in the puzzle. Look ➡ and ⬇.

could	more	every	leave	stop
just	money	once	ride	slow

j	n	a	e	c	c	n	x	o	d
x	d	x	r	o	z	g	z	s	a
p	f	b	z	u	s	t	o	p	g
b	z	e	c	l	m	r	c	f	k
o	z	v	s	d	o	i	f	k	c
n	t	e	l	k	n	d	l	q	g
c	b	r	o	s	e	e	e	x	b
e	g	y	w	k	y	b	a	u	n
u	j	u	s	t	h	s	v	x	e
e	o	e	m	o	r	e	e	o	v

Review

SORT the words. WRITE each word on a tower.

could   more   every   leave   stop

just   money   once   ride   slow

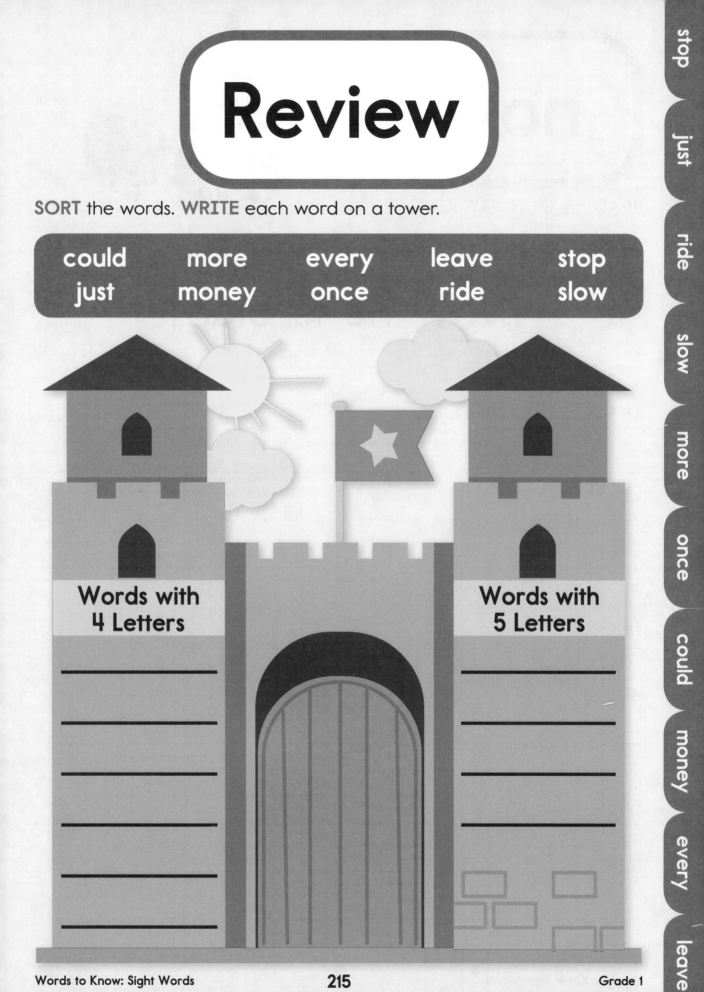

Words with
4 Letters

_____

_____

_____

_____

_____

Words with
5 Letters

_____

_____

_____

_____

_____

now

READ the word. SAY it out loud.

Now he is eight.

TRACE and WRITE the word.

last

time

soon

after

again

today

second

night

morning

FIND the word. Color the spaces with **now**.

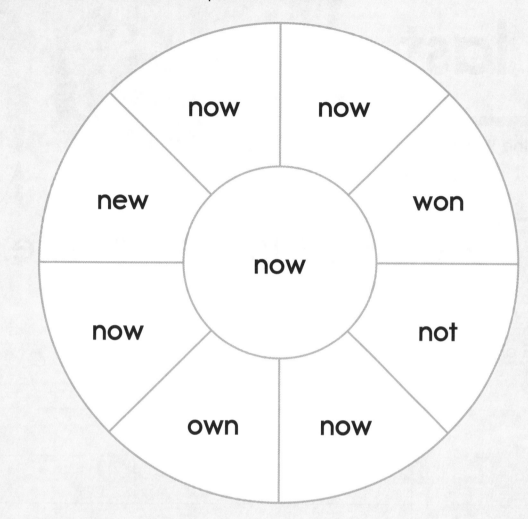

SPELL the word. Write the missing letters.

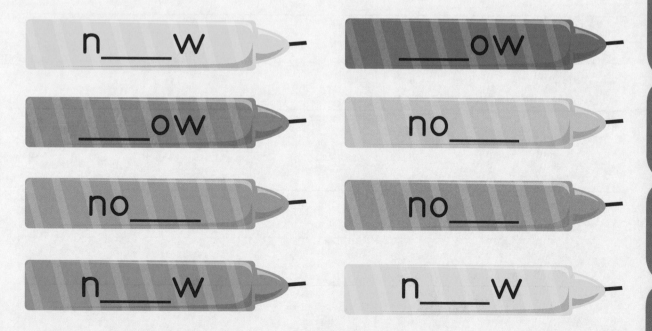

n___w

___ow

___ow

no___

no___

no___

n___w

n___w

now

last

time

soon

after

again

today

second

night

morning

now
last
time
soon
after
again
today
second
night
morning

last

READ the word. **SAY** it out loud.

The carrot is last in line.

TRACE and **WRITE** the word.

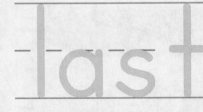

FIND the word. Circle **last**.

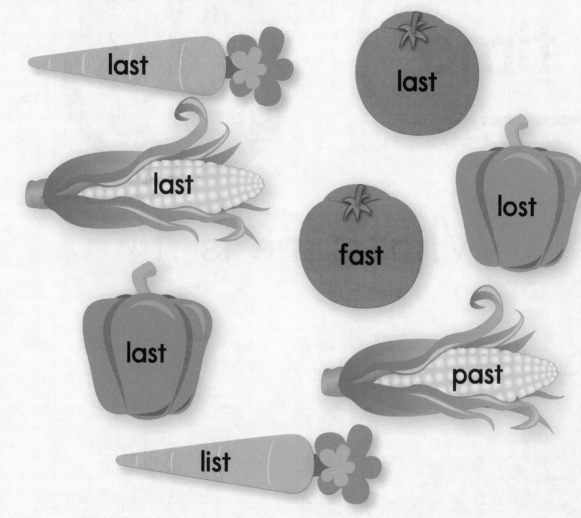

SPELL the word. Unscramble the letters to write **last**.

s a t l _____

t s l a _____

a t l s _____

t a s l _____

now

last

time

soon

after

again

today

second

night

morning

READ the word. **SAY** it out loud.

What time is it?

TRACE and **WRITE** the word.

FIND the word. Draw a line from the middle of the clock to **time**.
Use the color code to answer the riddle.

Why did the boy sit on a clock?

He wanted to be on _____ _____ _____ _____!

now

last

time

soon

after

again

today

second

night

morning

now

last

time

soon

after

again

today

second

night

morning

soon

READ the word. SAY it out loud.

She will land **soon**.

TRACE and WRITE the word.

FIND the word. Circle **soon** in each path.

SPELL the word. On each parachute, circle the letters in **soon**.

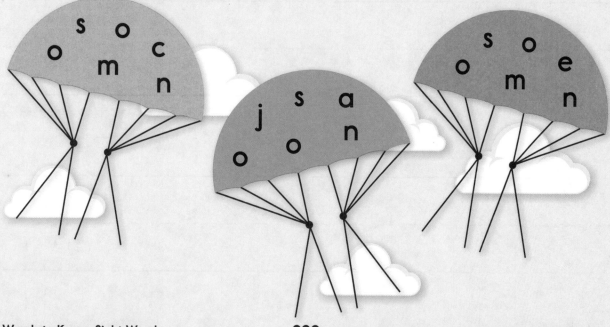

now

last

time

soon

after

again

today

second

night

morning

READ the word. **SAY** it out loud.

We clean up after dinner.

TRACE and **WRITE** the word.

after

SPELL the word. Match the letters in **after**.

aft

ter

afte

er

af

r

WRITE after to complete each sentence.

I am named _____ my father.

It is _____ three o'clock.

Can we have pie _____ lunch?

now

last

time

soon

after

again

today

second

night

morning

now
last
time
soon
after
again
today
second
night
morning

again

READ the word. **SAY** it out loud.

Do you want to play again?

TRACE and **WRITE** the word.

again

again

FIND the word. Circle **again** to see who wins the game.

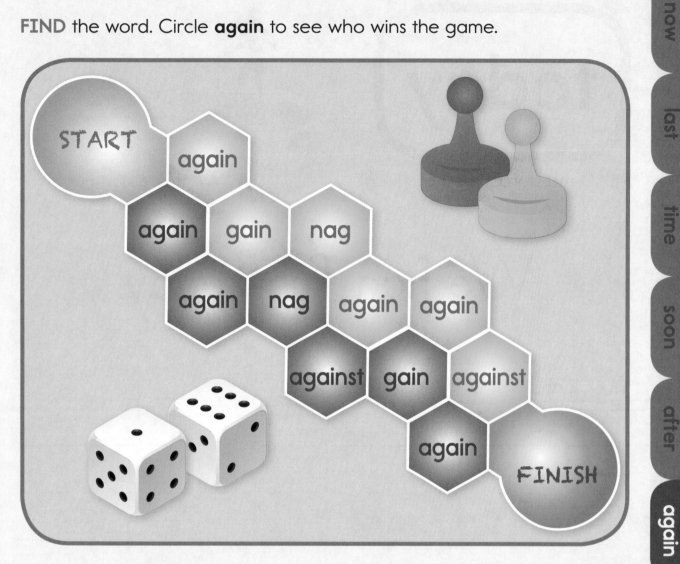

SPELL the word. Complete the word pyramids.

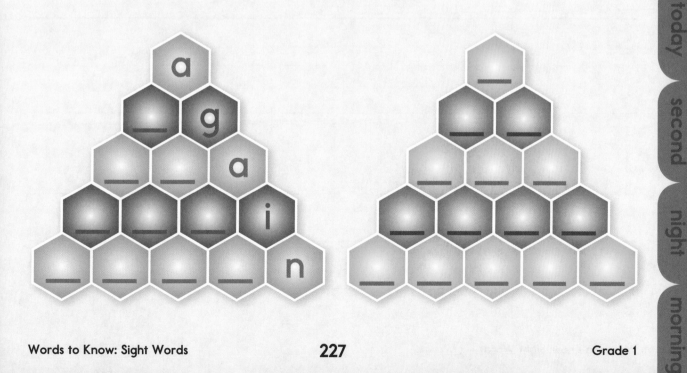

now

last

time

soon

after

again

today

second

night

morning

today

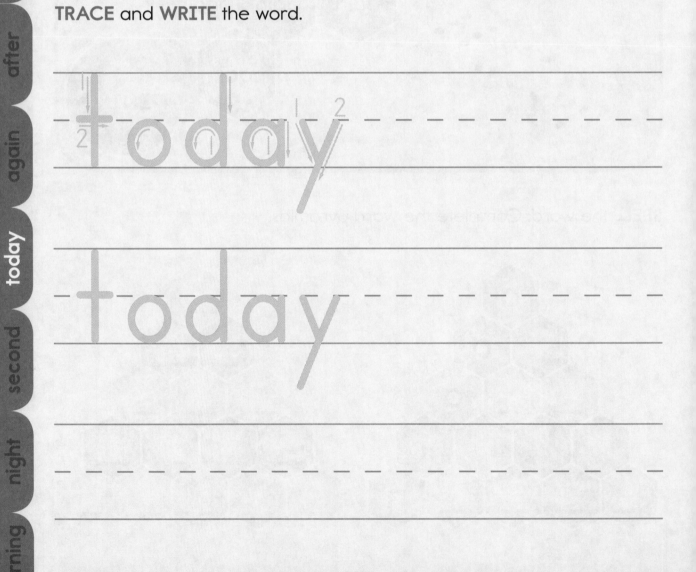

READ the word. **SAY** it out loud.

We had fun today.

TRACE and **WRITE** the word.

today

today

FIND the word. Circle **today**.

SPELL the word. Write **today** in the puzzle.

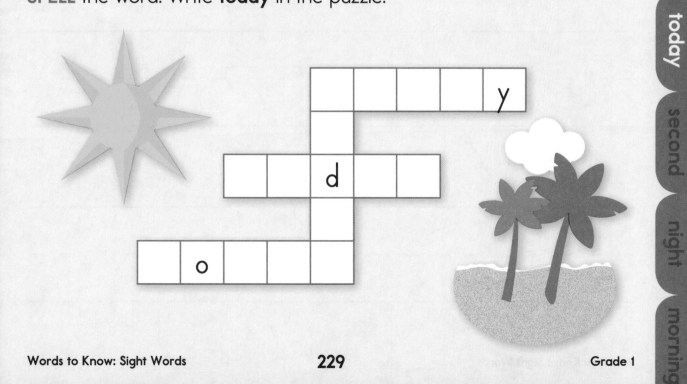

now
last
time
soon
after
again
today
second
night
morning

second

READ the word. SAY it out loud.

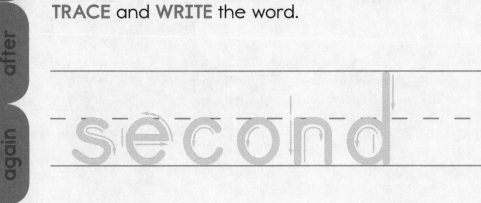

The **second** marble is red.

TRACE and WRITE the word.

second

second

SPELL the word. In each row, circle the letters in **second**. **WRITE** the word at the end of each row.

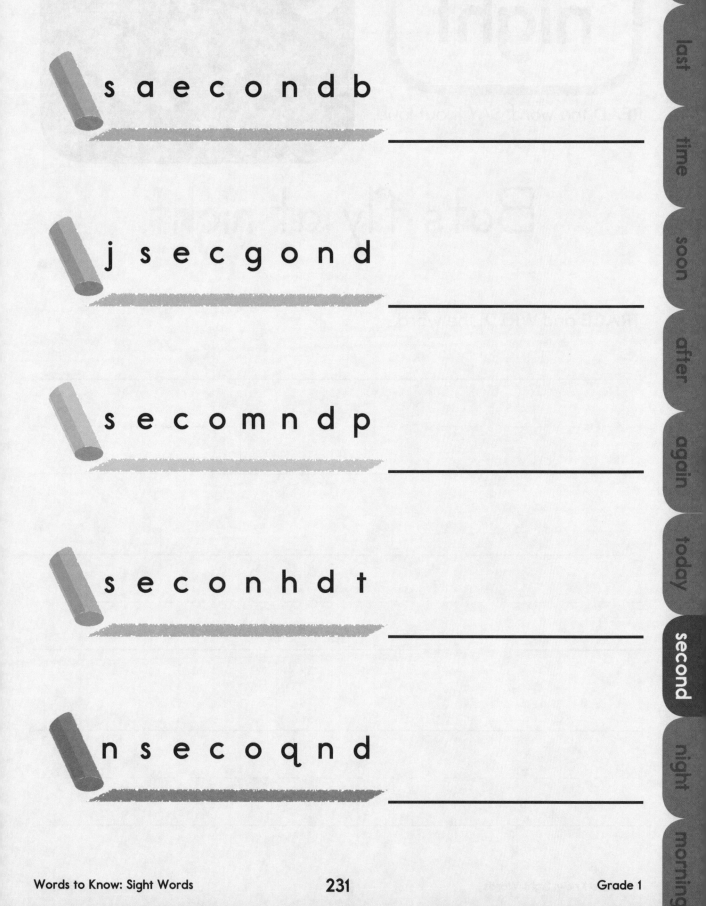

s a e c o n d b _____

j s e c g o n d _____

s e c o m n d p _____

s e c o n h d t _____

n s e c o q n d _____

now last time soon after again today second night morning

READ the word. **SAY** it out loud.

Bats fly at night.

TRACE and **WRITE** the word.

Sidebar tabs: now, last, time, soon, after, again, today, second, **night**, morning

FIND the word in the puzzle. Look → and ↓.

r	e	n	f	o
p	d	i	j	z
n	i	g	h	t
y	z	h	m	r
g	y	t	e	t

COUNT night and write the number. **COUNT** the words that rhyme with **night** and write the number.

night   Rhymes with **night**

___   ___

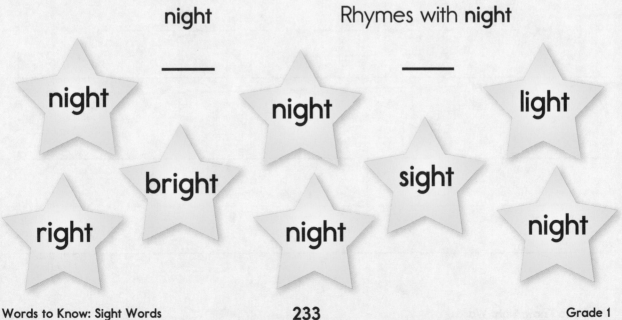

night

night   light

bright

right   night

sight

night   night

now last time soon after again today second night morning

morning

READ the word. **SAY** it out loud.

Birds chirp in the morning.

TRACE and **WRITE** the word.

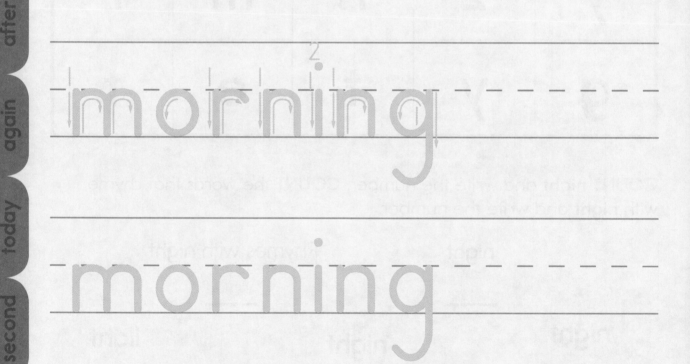

FIND the word. Color the spaces with **morning**.

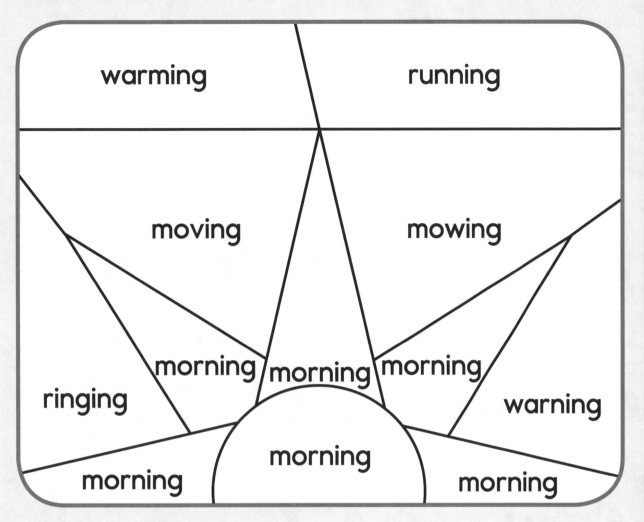

warming

running

moving

mowing

morning

morning

morning

ringing

warning

morning

morning

morning

SPELL the word. Circle each worm with **morning**.

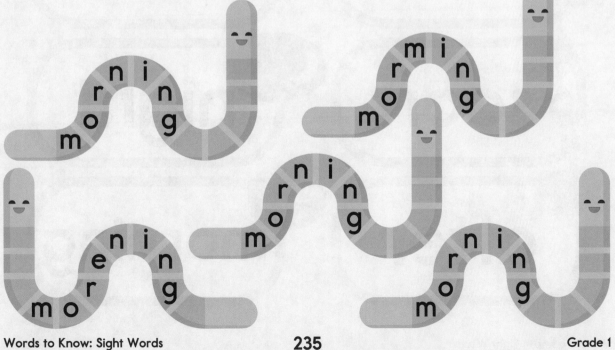

now
last
time
soon
after
again
today
second
night
morning

Review

READ the e-mail on the next page. FIND the 10 words. Circle each word you find.

now

again

last

today

time

second

soon

night

after

morning

Review

From: Marcus Kelly (mkelly@yahgoo.zom)

To: Nell Garvey (ngarvey@geemail.zom)

Date: July 26

Subject: Mammoth Cave!

Today we went to Mammoth Cave National Park. We had a great time! After we were in the cave, our tour guide turned out the lights. For a second, I was scared. It was so dark, I did not know if it was morning or night! Soon, the lights came back on again. We saw fish with no eyes. We saw fossils of animals that lived long ago. On the last part of the tour, we saw sparkly cave crystals. I attached a photo for you. We will be home from our trip any day now. I cannot wait to tell you more!

 Marcus

now · last · time · soon · after · again · today · second · night · morning

Review

WRITE words to finish the sentences.

| soon | today | night | time | now |

We slept all _____ in a tent.

Is it _____ for the show?

Summer cannot come _____ enough!

_____ is Thursday.

What are you doing right _____?

Dad will _____ the race.

It will _____ be midnight.

Review

WRITE words to finish the sentences.

last   after   again   second   morning

I hope we canoe _____ soon!

The _____ alphabet letter is B.

Who took the _____ cookie?

I woke up early this _____.

I play outside _____ school.

This will only take a _____.

How long does the game _____?

now   last   time   soon   after   again   today   second   night   morning

Review

GRAPH the words. Color one box for each word you count.

now   last   time   night   today
after   again   now   again
again   time   night   last
soon   after   time
second   night
second
night   last   time   time   morning

now					
last					
time					
soon					
after					
again					
today					
second					
night					
morning					

240

Review

CONNECT letters in each puzzle to spell three review words. WRITE the words on the lines. You will write two words more than once.

now
last
time
soon
after
again
today
second
night
morning

n	r	t	o
i	o	g	d
g	h	w	a
h	t	m	y

_____

_____

_____

m	o	r	n
a	n	o	i
f	z	w	n
t	e	r	g

_____

_____

_____

t	i	m	l
s	q	e	a
o	q	r	s
o	n	f	t

_____

_____

s	l	h	j
e	a	g	a
c	s	t	i
o	n	d	n

_____

_____

now
last
time
soon
after
again
today
second
night
morning

woman
kind
think
thing
sister
brother
should
please
know

man

READ the word. **SAY** it out loud.

My dad is a man.

TRACE and **WRITE** the word.

FIND the word. Circle **man** in each word.

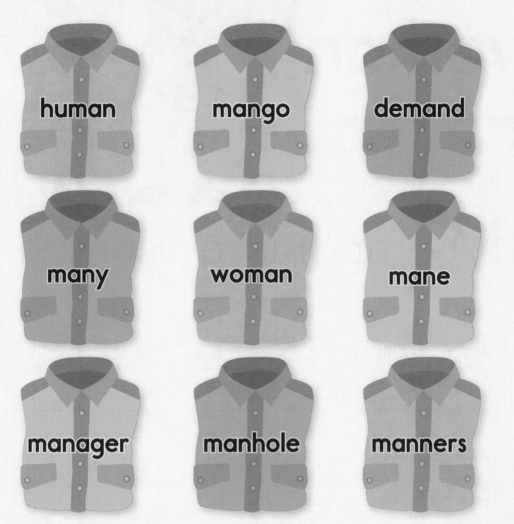

human

mango

demand

many

woman

mane

manager

manhole

manners

SPELL the word. Connect the letters in **man**.

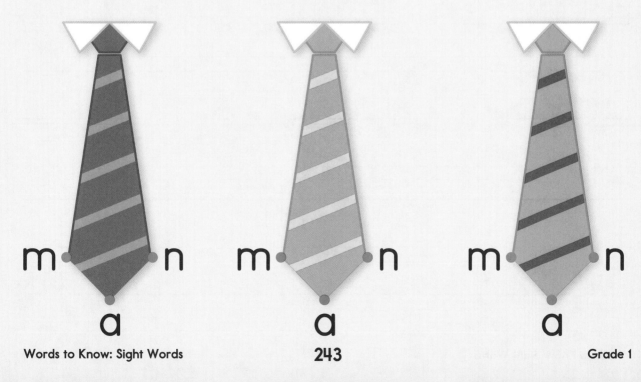

m   n

a

m   n

a

m   n

a

READ the word. **SAY** it out loud.

My mom is a woman.

TRACE and **WRITE** the word.

woman

woman

FIND the word. Color the spaces with **woman**.

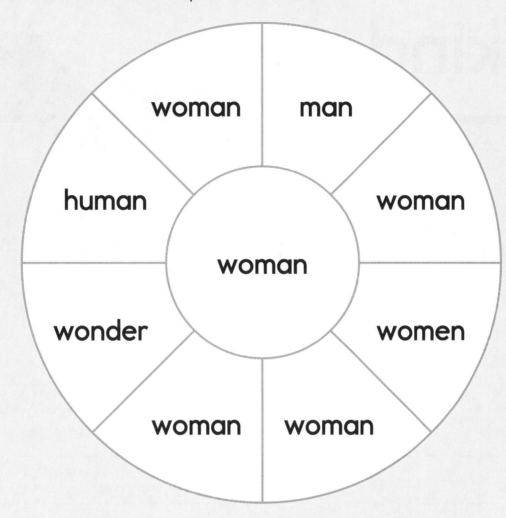

SPELL the word. Match the letters in **woman**.

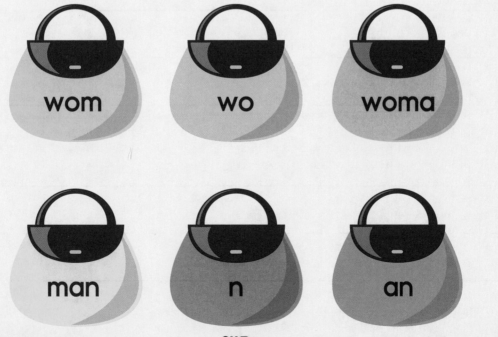

man
woman
kind
think
thing
sister
brother
should
please
know

man
woman
kind
think
thing
sister
brother
should
please
know

kind

READ the word. **SAY** it out loud.

What kind of bug is that?

TRACE and **WRITE** the word.

FIND the word. Circle **kind**.

SPELL the word. Circle **kind**.

kinde   kind   ciend

kind   kighnd   keind

cind   cynd   kind

man

woman

kind

think

thing

sister

brother

should

please

know

think

READ the word. **SAY** it out loud.

What do you think?

TRACE and **WRITE** the word.

think

think

FIND the word in the puzzle. Look → and ↓.

t	h	i	n	k
h	l	l	x	f
i	l	z	x	n
n	h	d	g	e
k	b	a	x	a

SPELL the word. Unscramble the letters to write **think**.

h k n
i t

_____

k i n
h t

_____

i t k
n h

_____

n i t
k h

_____

man

woman

kind

think

thing

sister

brother

should

please

know

thing

READ the word. **SAY** it out loud.

Which thing is hot?

TRACE and **WRITE** the word.

thing

thing

WRITE thing under the thing that is tall.

WRITE thing under the thing that is alive.

WRITE thing under the thing that is hard.

WRITE thing under the thing that is sharp.

man

woman

kind

think

thing

sister

brother

should

please

know

sister

READ the word. **SAY** it out loud.

My sister is a good cook.

TRACE and **WRITE** the word.

sister

FIND the word. Circle **sister**.

sister   mister   sister

sis   sister

sixteen   sister   sitter

SPELL the word. Circle **sister**.

sister   sistur   sistre

sister   sister

man
woman
kind
think
thing
sister
brother
should
please
know

man woman kind think thing sister brother should please know

brother

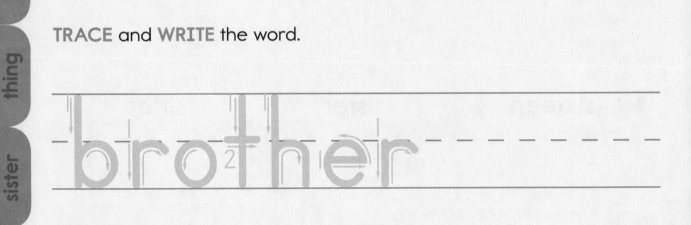

READ the word. **SAY** it out loud.

My brother swims well.

TRACE and **WRITE** the word.

brother

brother

COLOR each box with **brother**. Match each number to a letter to answer the riddle.

	e	r	e	i	e
5	brother	mother	bother	father	sister
4	broth	rather	bather	brother	both
3	bath	brother	baker	robber	there
2	mother	bother	brother	broth	rather
1	father	sister	bath	bather	brother

What is a good place to swim on Halloween?

Lake ___ ___ ___ ___ ___!
   1   2   3   4   5

man

woman

kind

think

thing

sister

brother

should

please

know

man
woman
kind
think
thing
sister
brother
should
please
know

should

READ the word. SAY it out loud.

We should sweep the floor.

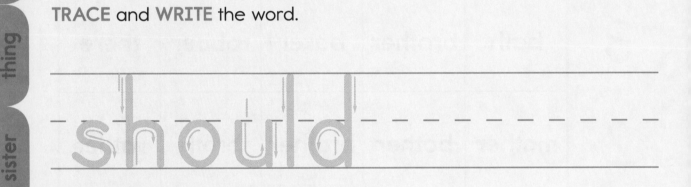

TRACE and WRITE the word.

should

should

FIND the word. Draw a line through **should** to see if you won!

should	should	should
hold	shoulder	could
would	loud	shout

SPELL the word. Write the missing letters.

s__o__ld

s__oul__

sh____ld

__hou__d

man

woman

kind

think

thing

sister

brother

should

please

know

man

woman

kind

think

thing

sister

brother

should

please

know

please

READ the word. **SAY** it out loud.

Please give me a roll.

TRACE and **WRITE** the word.

please

please

WRITE please to complete each sentence.

_____ help yourself to snacks.

Can I _____ go to the party?

It will _____ Mom to know
that I helped.

SPELL the word. Complete the word pyramids.

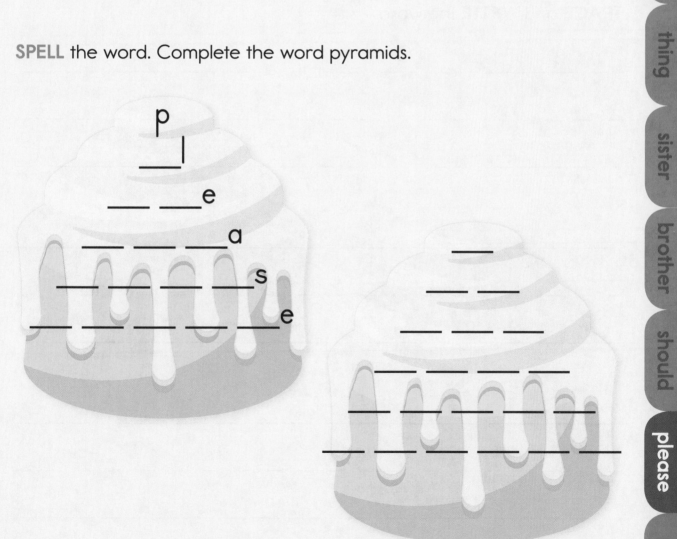

p
__ l
__ __ e
__ __ __ a
__ __ __ __ s
__ __ __ __ __ e

__
__ __
__ __ __
__ __ __ __
__ __ __ __ __
__ __ __ __ __ __

man
woman
kind
think
thing
sister
brother
should
please
know

man

woman

kind

think

thing

sister

brother

should

please

know

know

$24 + 3 = ?$

READ the word. SAY it out loud.

Do you know the answer?

TRACE and WRITE the word.

know

know

FIND the word. Color the spaces with **know**.

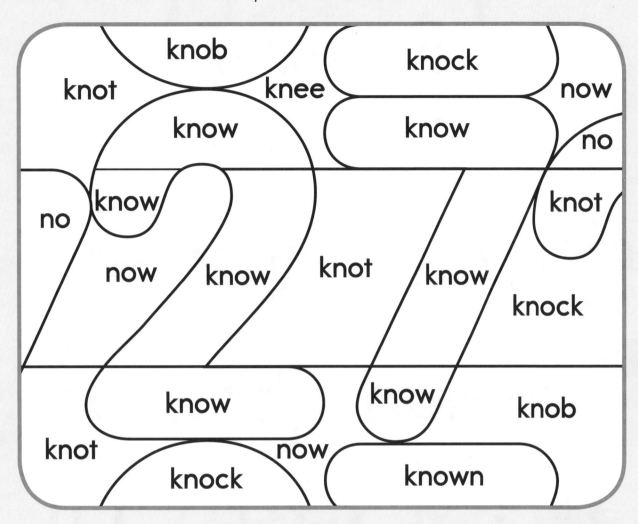

SPELL the word. In each puzzle, connect letters to spell **know**.

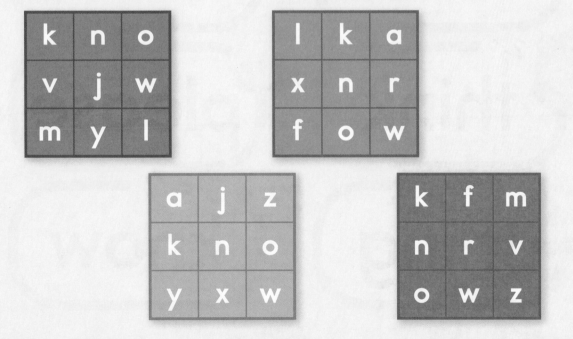

man

woman

kind

think

thing

sister

brother

should

please

know

Review

READ the story on the next page. FIND the 10 words. Circle each word you find.

man

sister

woman

brother

kind

should

think

please

thing

24 + 3 = ?

know

Review

Super Artist

"What are you drawing?" my sister asked.

"A new superhero," I said.

"Is it a man or a woman?"

"Not a woman or a man. I think it will be a thing that has come to life. Maybe a giant storm cloud."

"Cool! Your hero should have a superpower. What kind of power will it be?"

"I know! My cloud hero will use rain, wind, and lightning to fight villains."

"You have a super imagination, little brother," my sister said. "Can I please see your picture when it is done?"

"It will be done in a super-second!" I promised.

man

woman

kind

think

thing

sister

brother

should

please

know

man

woman

kind

think

thing

sister

brother

should

please

know

Review

WRITE words to finish the sentences.

| know | man | sister | please | thing |

My _____ is younger than me.

That _____ is our neighbor.

_____ pass the butter.

I _____ lots of sight words!

I need one _____ from the store.

The visit will _____ Grandma.

I _____ lots of people here.

Review

WRITE words to finish the sentences.

woman   kind   brother   think   should

My _____ is older than me.

That _____ is mom's friend.

Always be _____ to others.

I _____ do my homework.

What did you _____ of the movie?

That _____ of candy is my favorite.

_____ we go today or tomorrow?

Review

WRITE the missing letters. Use the code to help you.

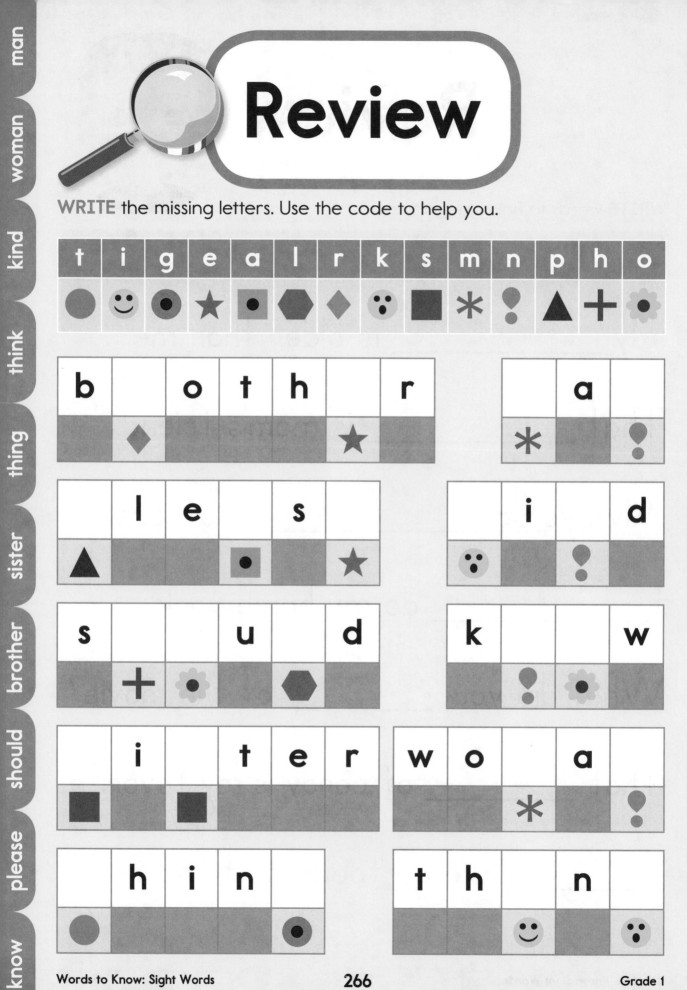

Review

WRITE letters to complete the words. Use the color code to finish the joke.

man	kind	thing	brother	please
woman	think	sister	should	know

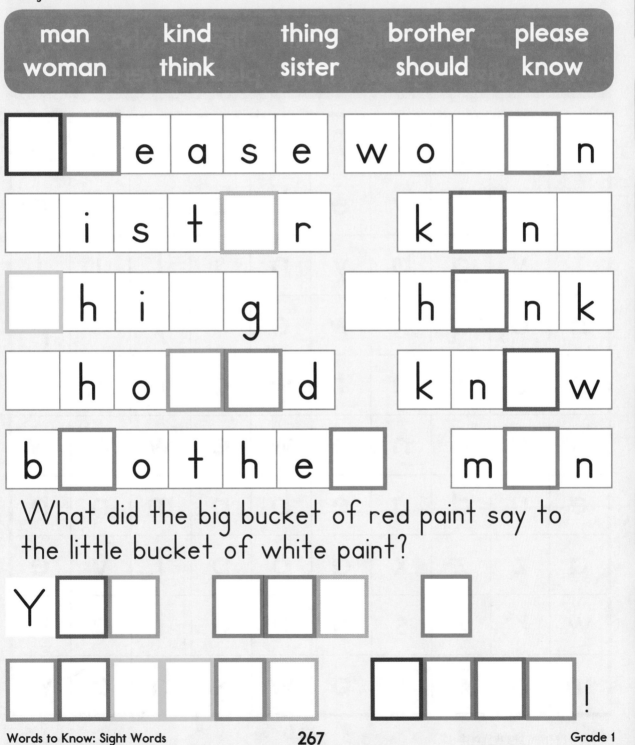

□ □ e a s e   w o □ n

□ i s t □ r   k □ n

□ h i □ g   h □ n k

h o □ □ d   k n □ w

b □ o t h e □   m □ n

What did the big bucket of red paint say to the little bucket of white paint?

Y □ □   □ □ □   □

□ □ □ □ □ □   □ □ □ □ !

Sight Words Review

FIND rhyming words. Read each sight word. Find a rhyming sight word in the puzzle. Look → and ↓.

pet	any	would	slow	then	who	by
wish	give	grow	how	please	were	

f	b	j	t	f	f	i	s	h	o
a	l	i	v	e	k	z	f	f	e
t	v	g	b	y	n	s	l	j	l
h	o	q	k	w	o	h	y	c	p
e	b	l	e	t	w	o	r	m	k
s	q	d	n	o	w	e	w	a	w
e	u	d	u	e	b	p	m	n	h
a	z	z	x	q	p	b	l	y	e
w	k	z	s	h	o	u	l	d	n
m	h	e	r	p	w	s	h	o	w

Sight Words Review

FIND the words. Circle two words that fit each category. Win the race!

Has short a
may
ask
last

Has double consonants
happy
soon
pretty

Has long i
night
kind
thing

Has short u
put
just
went

Has an
want
name
woman

Has two syllables
round
money
brother

Has long e
each
ride
leave

Has consonant blend
present
stop
under

FINISH

Sight Words Review

WRITE the letter on each paint can to complete a group of words. Use the color code.

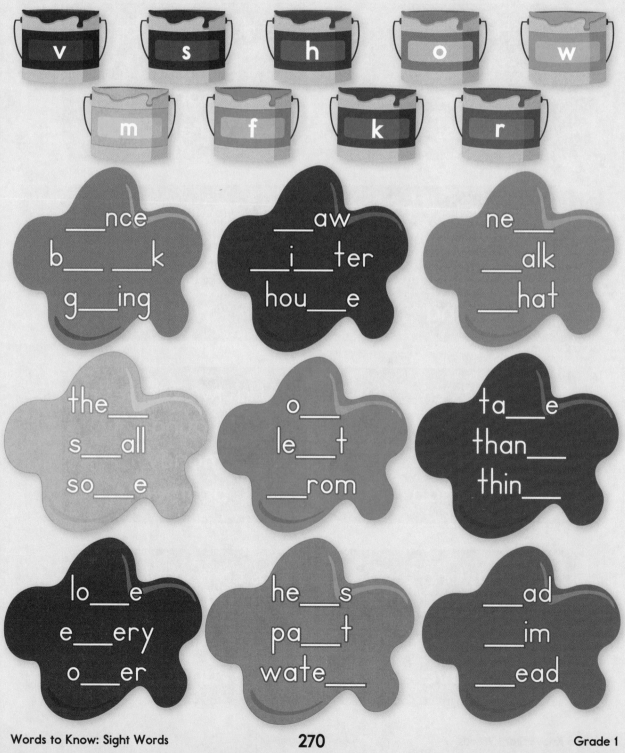

v   s   h   o   w

m   f   k   r

___nce
b___ ___k
g___ing

___aw
___i___ter
hou___e

ne___
___alk
___hat

the___
s___all
so___e

o___
le___t
___rom

ta___e
than___
thin___

lo___e
e___ery
o___er

he___s
pa___t
wate___

___ad
___im
___ead

Sight Words Review

WRITE the letter on each paint can to complete a group of words. Use the color code.

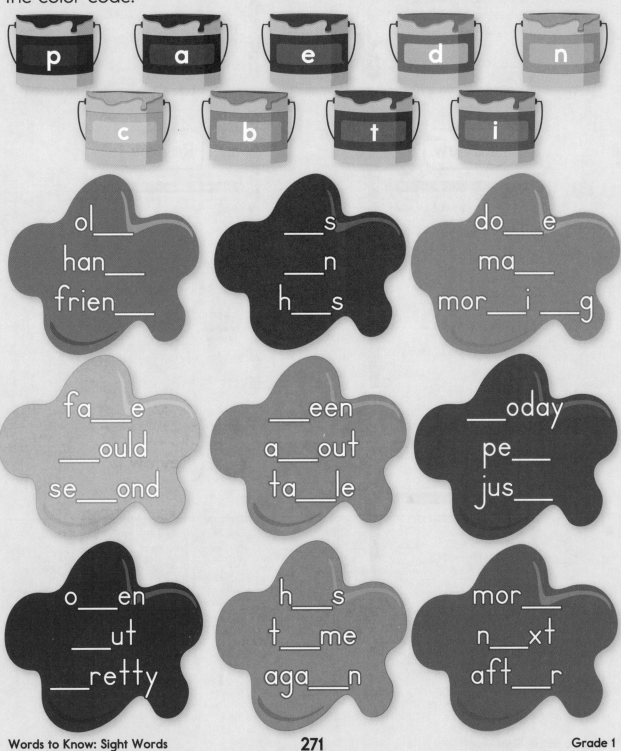

p   a   e   d   n

c   b   t   i

ol___
han___
frien___

___s
___n
h___s

do___e
ma___
mor___i___g

fa___e
___ould
se___ond

___een
a___out
ta___le

___oday
pe___
jus___

o___en
___ut
___retty

h___s
t___me
aga___n

mor___
n___xt
aft___r

Words to Know: Sight Words

Grade 1

Page 29

Review

What Pet?

"Dad," I said, "I (want) (a) (new) (pet.)"

"What kind (of) (pet?)" asked Dad.

"I (want) (a) (pet) that I have never (had) before."

"So, not a stuffed animal. You have lots (of) those," Dad joked.

"No! I (want) (a) real animal. (An) animal that will let me (pet) (it) as much as I (want.)"

"So, not a rhino," Dad teased.

"No! I (want) (a) (pet) that I can (put) in my lap."

"How about a puppy?" asked Dad.

"Yes! I would (love) to get a puppy!"

Words to Know: Sight Words   29   Grade 1

29

Page 30

Review

WRITE words to finish the sentences.

| want | put | pet | an | of |

Joey has a _pet_ goldfish in a bowl.

I drank a glass _of_ lemonade.

Do you _want_ to play a game?

Sari _put_ on her hat and gloves.

Would you like a pear or _an_ apple?

I _pet_ the rabbit's soft fur.

Dad has a fear _of_ high places.

Words to Know: Sight Words   30   Grade 1

30

Page 31

Review

WRITE words to finish the sentences.

| as | let | had | new | love |

I got _new_ clothes for school.

Will your mom _let_ you come over?

This worm is _as_ long _as_ my hand.

I told Grandma that I _love_ her.

We _had_ chicken for dinner.

Let this string hang down.

January begins a _new_ year.

Words to Know: Sight Words   31   Grade 1

31

Page 32

Review

SORT the words. WRITE each word on a cone.

want pet an put as let had new of love

Words with 2 Letters: an, as, of

Words with 3 Letters: put, let, pet, new, had

Words with 4 Letters: love, want

Words to Know: Sight Words   32   Grade 1

32

Page 33

Review

WRITE a word in the puzzle to complete each sentence.

want pet an put as let had new of love

DOWN
1. Do you see ___ orange crayon?
3. What movie do you ___ to watch?
5. Izzy is my ___ iguana.
7. Mom and Dad ___ me.

ACROSS
2. I need ___ shoes.
4. Come as soon ___ you can.
5. I ___ a dollar in my pocket.
6. We ___ fun last week.
7. Please ___ the dog out.
8. This is a book ___ stories.

Crossword answers: ¹a, ²new, ³as, ⁵put, ⁶had, ⁷let, ⁸of, love

Words to Know: Sight Words   33   Grade 1

33

Page 55

Review

Which Kid?

(Her) old toy is (by) (her.) It (has) been (hers) since she was four years old.

(He) (has) (part) (of) (his) sweet snack. (He) (may) eat the rest later.

He likes to learn about dinosaurs. (His) teacher gave (him) a (book) to read.

Words to Know: Sight Words   55   Grade 1

55

56

Review

WRITE words to finish the sentences.

| book | her | has | by | may |

The elephant __has__ two tusks.

Mom asked me to hold __her__ purse.

I checked out a library __book__.

I sat __by__ Marius and Ethan on the bus.

We __may__ go to the pool today.

Did you __book__ our hotel room?

This book is __by__ Barbara Park.

Words to Know: Sight Words 56 Grade 1

57

Review

WRITE words to finish the sentences.

| old | him | part | his | hers |

You can have __part__ of my cookie.

My brother lost __his__ tooth.

I am seven years __old__.

Carlos asked me to play with __him__.

Bella said the backpack is __hers__.

This __old__ blanket has a hole in it.

Mari got a __part__ in the play.

Words to Know: Sight Words 57 Grade 1

58

Review

COLOR the words that are spelled correctly. WRITE letters to complete the words.

b o_ ok   ha s_

p_ a r t_   b y_

h e_ rs   o_ l d

h_ is   ma y_

h_ im   h e_ r

Words to Know: Sight Words 58 Grade 1

59

Review

GRAPH the words. Color one box for each word you count.

by					
him					
her					
hers					
his					
has					
may					
old					
book					
part					

Words to Know: Sight Words 59 Grade 1

81

Review

Jumping In

Robert (saw) that (many) kids (were) already in. He jumped in, too. The water was cold for (these) early lessons! (Any) time now, class would start. Robert watched the teacher (show) what to do. He put his (face) in the water. He moved his (head) to the side to breathe. He dragged his (hand) through the water as he kicked. He (went) forward a little bit in the pool. Robert was doing it! He was swimming!

Words to Know: Sight Words 81 Grade 1

82

Review

WRITE words to finish the sentences.

| show | these | face | any | saw |

We __saw__ a pretty bird.

Anita had a smile on her __face__.

__These__ snacks are for the party.

Let me __show__ you what I made!

Do you have __any__ good ideas?

Sam decided to __face__ his problem.

We need a hammer and a __saw__.

Words to Know: Sight Words 82 Grade 1

Page 83

Review

WRITE words to finish the sentences.

| hand | were | many | head | went |

__Many__ chickens live in this coop.

Hold the umbrella over your __head__.

I held a worm in my __hand__.

My friends __were__ so nice to me!

He __went__ to camp last summer.

We are going to __head__ home.

Please __hand__ me the envelope.

Words to Know: Sight Words 83 Grade 1

83

Page 84

Review

FIND the words in the puzzle. Look → and ↓.

| these | face | went | show | hand |
| head | many | were | any | saw |

k	w	e	n	t	p	f	r	m	s
h	o	u	w	m	a	n	y	y	j
n	f	v	j	d	p	j	x	q	a
z	a	d	h	r	w	n	t	c	o
b	c	n	t	h	e	s	e	t	f
s	e	b	k	z	r	p	h	c	a
h	j	t	k	e	e	q	d	z	n
o	e	p	f	j	h	a	n	d	y
w	g	r	g	h	e	a	d	d	k
j	k	s	a	w	m	l	j	p	x

Words to Know: Sight Words 84 Grade 1

84

Page 85

Review

MATCH the words. Use the codes to complete the jokes.

1. head — show
2. face — any
3. many — head
4. show — many
5. any — face

What do you call an old snowman?
__w a t e r__!
 1 2 3 4 5

1. these — hand
2. went — these
3. saw — were
4. were — saw
5. hand — went

How do you know that the ocean is
friendly? It __w a v e s__!
 1 2 3 4 5

Words to Know: Sight Words 85 Grade 1

85

Page 107

Review

Hermit Crabs

The (next) time you are by the ocean, look for a shell that seems to (walk) by itself. It could be a live hermit crab (going) across the sand. Hermit crabs have ten legs and two (claws). The left claw is larger. It can be used as a weapon.

Hermit crabs have soft bodies that need protection. So, they look for an old shell that they can use (over) again as a (house). Just like you need a new (shoe) when your foot grows, hermit crabs need larger shells as they get bigger. When they are (done) with one shell, they look for a new one. Hermit crabs have (been) seen fighting each other for better shells.

Words to Know: Sight Words 107 Grade 1

107

Page 108

Review

WRITE words to finish the sentences.

| over | been | going | next | shoe |

I am __going__ to win the race!

It has __been__ a long day.

I need to tie my __shoe__.

Is the movie __over__ yet?

I am __next__ in line.

How have you __been__ lately?

Where is Ben __going__?

Words to Know: Sight Words 108 Grade 1

108

Page 109

Review

WRITE words to finish the sentences.

| walk | live | house | left | done |

I am __done__ with my dinner.

We will __walk__ at the park.

That is a real __live__ raccoon.

I scraped my __left__ knee.

This is my friend's __house__.

I __live__ on the next block.

The birds have __left__ the nest.

Words to Know: Sight Words 109 Grade 1

109

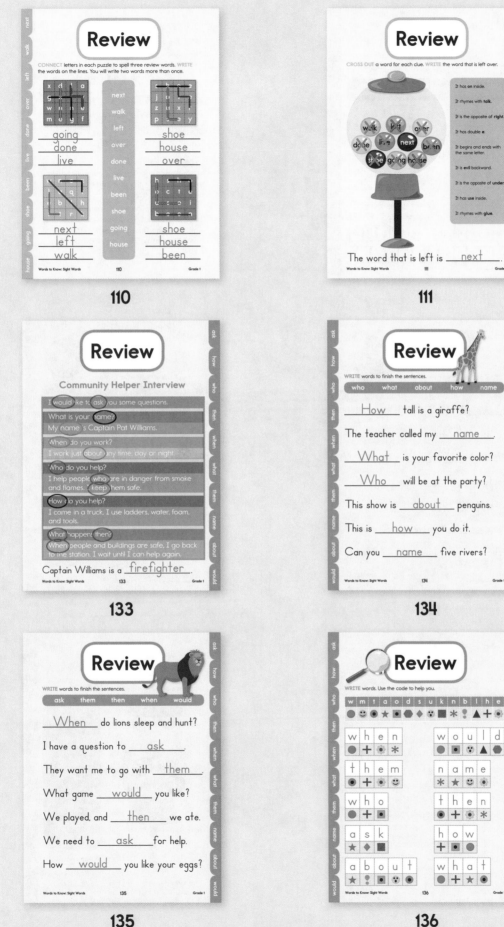

110

111

133

134

135

136

137

Review

WRITE letters to complete the words. Use the color code to finish the joke.

ask	who	when	them	about
how	then	what	name	would

w h e n	a s k
n a m e	t h e n
a b o u t	w h o
h o w	t h e m
w h a t	w o u l d

When do you go at red and stop at green?

w h e n   y o u   e a t

w a t e r m e l o n s !

Words to Know: Sight Words   137   Grade 1

159

Review

Wishing for Fish

Sadie sat on the dock. She tried to see under the water. Were some fish down there?

Sadie saw a small ripple on the water. Was that a fish? No, it was only a fly.

Then, Sadie saw some round rings on the water. She watched each circle grow bigger and bigger. Was that a fish? She heard her brother laugh. When she looked up, she saw him tossing rocks into the water. "Stop it!" she said. "Come help me look for a fish."

Bryce sat by Sadie. They were both quiet. Suddenly, a seagull swooped down. The kids watched the bird take a floppy thing from the water. "I know what that was!" said Sadie. "I saw a fish!"

Words to Know: Sight Words   159   Grade 1

160

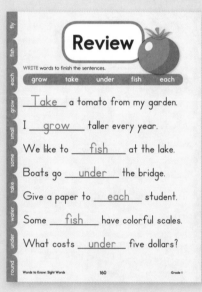

Review

WRITE words to finish the sentences.

grow	take	under	fish	each

Take a tomato from my garden.

I _grow_ taller every year.

We like to _fish_ at the lake.

Boats go _under_ the bridge.

Give a paper to _each_ student.

Some _fish_ have colorful scales.

What costs _under_ five dollars?

Words to Know: Sight Words   160   Grade 1

161

Review   1¢

WRITE words to finish the sentences.

fly	small	some	water	round

A penny has a _round_ shape.

All plants need _water_.

I ordered a _small_ popcorn.

This chore will take _some_ time.

Bats are mammals that can _fly_.

Please _round_ up all the crayons.

Water the garden each week.

Words to Know: Sight Words   161   Grade 1

162

Review

WRITE a word in the puzzle to complete each sentence.

fly	each	small	take	under
fish	grow	some	water	round

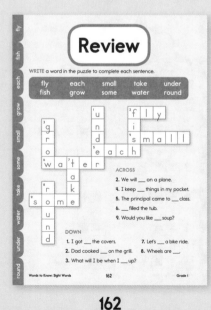

Crossword answers:
- ¹u n d e r
- ²f l y
- g r o w
- ⁴s m a l l
- i n d e e d / e a c h
- w a ⁴t e r
- r a k e
- ⁹s o m e
- r o u n d

ACROSS

2. We will ___ on a plane.
4. I keep ___ things in my pocket.
5. The principal came to ___ class.
6. ___ filled the tub.
9. Would you like ___ soup?

DOWN

1. I got ___ the covers.   7. Let's ___ a bike ride.
2. Dad cooked ___ on the grill. 8. Wheels are ___.
3. What will I be when I ___ up?

Words to Know: Sight Words   162   Grade 1

163

Review

CROSS OUT a word for each clue. WRITE the word that is left over.

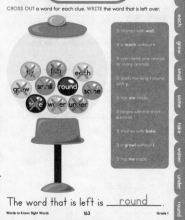

- It rhymes with wall.
- It is teach without t.
- It can name one animal or many animals.
- It spells the long i sound with y.
- It has ate inside.
- It begins with the short u sound.
- It rhymes with bake.
- It is growl without l.
- It has me inside.

The word that is left is _round_.

Words to Know: Sight Words   163   Grade 1

185

Review

Things to Do at My Birthday Party

- [ ] Put (pretty) decorations on the (table.)
- [ ] Say hello to each (friend)
- [ ] Play fun games!
- [ ] Sing (Happy) Birthday. Blow out the candles and make a (wish.)
- [ ] (Open) presents. Ask who each (present) is (from.) Thank the giver.
- [ ] (Give) a treat to each (friend.)

Words to Know: Sight Words   185   Grade 1

186

Review

WRITE words to finish the sentences.

| thank | present | wish | pretty | table |

You have a ___pretty___ cat.

All 20 students are ___present___ .

I ___wish___ I could see you.

We do crafts at the ___table___ .

___Thank___ you for helping me!

This is a ___present___ for you.

That is a ___pretty___ tall tree!

Words to Know: Sight Words   186   Grade 1

187

Review

WRITE words to finish the sentences.

| happy | give | from | friend | open |

The letter is ___from___ Reggie.

Reggie is my ___friend___ .

His family is ___from___ Florida.

I cannot wait to ___open___ the letter.

I am ___happy___ to hear from him!

I will ___give___ him a picture I made.

I hope it will make him ___happy___ .

Words to Know: Sight Words   187   Grade 1

188

Review

MATCH the words. Use the codes to complete the jokes.

1. friend — give   e
2. give — open   c
3. thank — present   e
4. present — friend   f
5. open — thank   n

What runs around the yard while standing still? A f e n c e !
1 2 3 4 5

1. wish — table   o
2. happy — pretty   c
3. table — wish   c
4. pretty — from   k
5. from — happy   l

What has a face and hands, but no arms and legs? A c l o c k !
1 2 3 4 5

Words to Know: Sight Words   188   Grade 1

189

Review

COLOR the words that are spelled correctly. WRITE letters to complete the words.

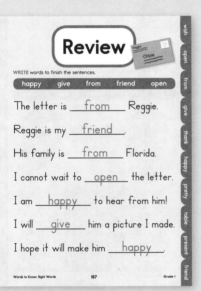

happy, wish, freind, give, happe, pretty, thanke, opun, present, open, giv, table, tabel, from, frum, thank, wissh, friend, pritty, prasent

t a b l e   tha n k

w i sh   ha p p y

o p e n   pr e tt y

f r iend   giv e

fr o m   p r es ent

Words to Know: Sight Words   189   Grade 1

211

Review

Piggy Bank Craft

Make a piggy bank! (Just) find an empty plastic bottle, colored paper, scissors, glue, four bottle lids, a pipe cleaner, and a knife.

Ask an adult to use the knife to cut a slit in the bottle. (Stop) when it is big enough for a quarter. (Once) that is done, cut ears, eyes, and a nose from paper. (Slow) down and think of (more) ideas. You (could) make a surfboard for your pig to (ride) or glasses for it to wear. Glue the paper on the bottle. (Leave) space so you can glue on the lids to make feet. Add a pipe cleaner tail, too.

Do not forget to put (money) in your bank (every) day!

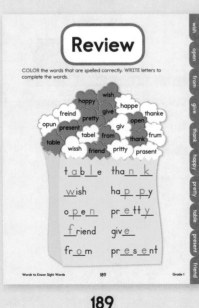

Words to Know: Sight Words   211   Grade 1

212

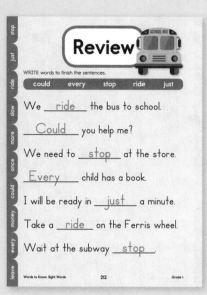

Review

WRITE words to finish the sentences.

| could | every | stop | ride | just |

We __ride__ the bus to school.

__Could__ you help me?

We need to __stop__ at the store.

__Every__ child has a book.

I will be ready in __just__ a minute.

Take a __ride__ on the Ferris wheel.

Wait at the subway __stop__ .

Words to Know: Sight Words · 212 · Grade 1

212

213

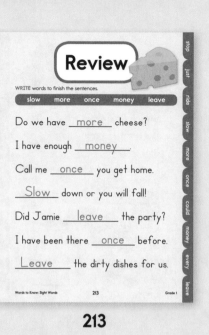

Review

WRITE words to finish the sentences.

| slow | more | once | money | leave |

Do we have __more__ cheese?

I have enough __money__ .

Call me __once__ you get home.

__Slow__ down or you will fall!

Did Jamie __leave__ the party?

I have been there __once__ before.

__Leave__ the dirty dishes for us.

Words to Know: Sight Words · 213 · Grade 1

213

214

Review

FIND the words in the puzzle. Look → and ↓.

| could | more | every | leave | stop |
| just | money | once | ride | slow |

j	n	a	e	c	c	n	x	o	d
x	d	x	r	o	z	g	z	s	a
p	f	b	z	u	s	t	o	p	g
b	z	e	c	l	m	r	c	f	k
o	z	v	s	d	o	i	f	k	c
n	t	e	l	k	n	d	l	q	g
c	b	r	o	s	e	e	e	x	b
e	g	y	w	k	y	b	a	u	n
u	j	u	s	t	h	s	v	x	e
e	o	e	m	o	r	e	e	o	v

Words to Know: Sight Words · 214 · Grade 1

214

215

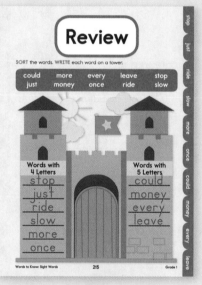

Review

SORT the words. WRITE each word on a tower.

| could | more | every | leave | stop |
| just | money | once | ride | slow |

Words with 4 Letters
stop
just
ride
slow
more
once

Words with 5 Letters
could
money
every
leave

Words to Know: Sight Words · 215 · Grade 1

215

237

Review

From: Marcus Kelly (mkelly@yahgoo.zom)

To: Nell Garvey (ngarvey@geemail.zom)

Date: July 26

Subject: Mammoth Cave!

(Today) we went to Mammoth Cave National Park. We had a great (time.) (After) we were in the cave, our tour guide turned out the lights. For a (second) I was scared. It was so dark, I did not know if it was (morning) or (night.) (Soon) the lights came back on (again.) We saw fish with no eyes. We saw fossils of animals that lived long ago. On the (last) part of the tour, we saw sparkly cave crystals. I attached a photo for you. We will be home from our trip any day (now.) I cannot wait to tell you more!

☺ Marcus

Words to Know: Sight Words · 237 · Grade 1

237

238

Review

WRITE words to finish the sentences.

| soon | today | night | time | now |

We slept all __night__ in a tent.

Is it __time__ for the show?

Summer cannot come __soon__ enough!

__Today__ is Thursday.

What are you doing right __now__ ?

Dad will __time__ the race.

It will __soon__ be midnight.

Words to Know: Sight Words · 238 · Grade 1

238

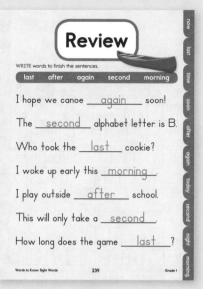

239

Review

WRITE words to finish the sentences.

last after again second morning

I hope we canoe __again__ soon!

The __second__ alphabet letter is B.

Who took the __last__ cookie?

I woke up early this __morning__.

I play outside __after__ school.

This will only take a __second__.

How long does the game __last__?

Words to Know: Sight Words   239   Grade 1

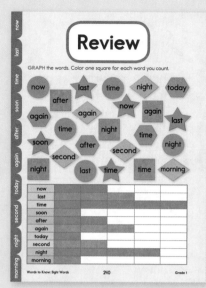

240

Review

GRAPH the words. Color one square for each word you count.

now	last	time	night	today
after		now	again	last
again	again	night		
time	night	time		
soon	after	second	night	
second				
night	last	time	time	morning

now					
last					
time					
soon					
after					
again					
today					
second					
night					
morning					

Words to Know: Sight Words   240   Grade 1

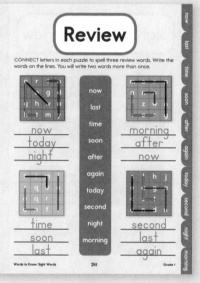

241

Review

CONNECT letters in each puzzle to spell three review words. Write the words on the lines. You will write two words more than once.

now
last
time
soon
after
again
today
second
night
morning

__now__
__today__
__night__

__morning__
__after__
__now__

__time__
__soon__
__last__

__second__
__last__
__again__

Words to Know: Sight Words   241   Grade 1

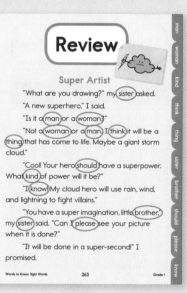

263

Review

Super Artist

"What are you drawing?" my (sister) asked.

"A new superhero," I said.

"Is it a (man) or a (woman)?"

"Not a (woman) or a (man). I (think) it will be a (thing) that has come to life. Maybe a giant storm cloud."

"Cool! Your hero (should) have a superpower. What (kind) of power will it be?"

"I (know)! My cloud hero will use rain, wind, and lightning to fight villains."

"You have a super imagination, little (brother)," my (sister) said. "Can I (please) see your picture when it is done?"

"It will be done in a super-second!" I promised.

Words to Know: Sight Words   263   Grade 1

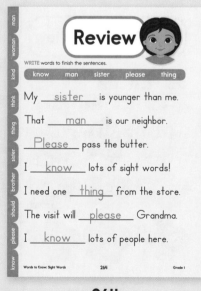

264

Review

WRITE words to finish the sentences.

know man sister please thing

My __sister__ is younger than me.

That __man__ is our neighbor.

__Please__ pass the butter.

I __know__ lots of sight words!

I need one __thing__ from the store.

The visit will __please__ Grandma.

I __know__ lots of people here.

Words to Know: Sight Words   264   Grade 1

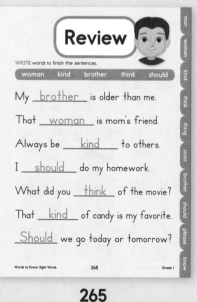

265

Review

WRITE words to finish the sentences.

woman kind brother think should

My __brother__ is older than me.

That __woman__ is mom's friend.

Always be __kind__ to others.

I __should__ do my homework.

What did you __think__ of the movie?

That __kind__ of candy is my favorite.

__Should__ we go today or tomorrow?

Words to Know: Sight Words   265   Grade 1

266

267

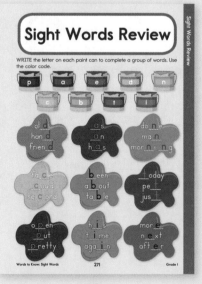

268

269

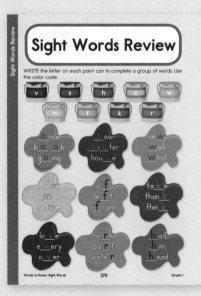

270

271

Sight Words Flash Cards

A flash card is provided for each word taught in this book. Help your child cut apart the flash cards. Store the cards in a zip-top bag. You may wish to laminate the cards or copy them onto card stock.

Use the cards for a variety of hands-on learning activities. Try these ideas:

Use the color-coded borders to find the 10 word cards that match each section of this book. As your child works through the pages of the section, he or she can match the cards to the activities.

Use the category cards on page 317 to sort all the cards according to how many letters they have.

Put the cards together in different ways to form simple phrases, sentences, and stories.

Find the cards with words that your child can read easily and put them in an envelope. Count those cards and write the number on the envelope. Then, work with the remaining cards each day, moving them into the envelope as your child learns the words. Keep changing the number on the envelope until it says 100!

Spread out 10 to 20 cards face-up. Can your child find pairs of rhyming words? Look at the letters in the rhyming words. Which letters are the same?

Turn any 12 cards facedown and arrange them in a grid. Ask your child to turn over any two cards and read the words. Can he or she find one way that the words are alike? Do they share letters, have the same number of letters, or have similar meanings? If so, your child keeps the cards. If not, turn the cards over. Keep going until your child has all the cards.

Use the cards to play Go Fish. On each turn, ask the other player for a card with a word that has a certain characteristic. For example, say, "Do you have a word with the letter **o**?", "Do you have a word with four letters?", or "Do you have a word that names a person?" If the answer is no, go fish!

Choose any 10 cards. Then, read a storybook together. Can you find each word in the book?

an

as

of

put

let

pet

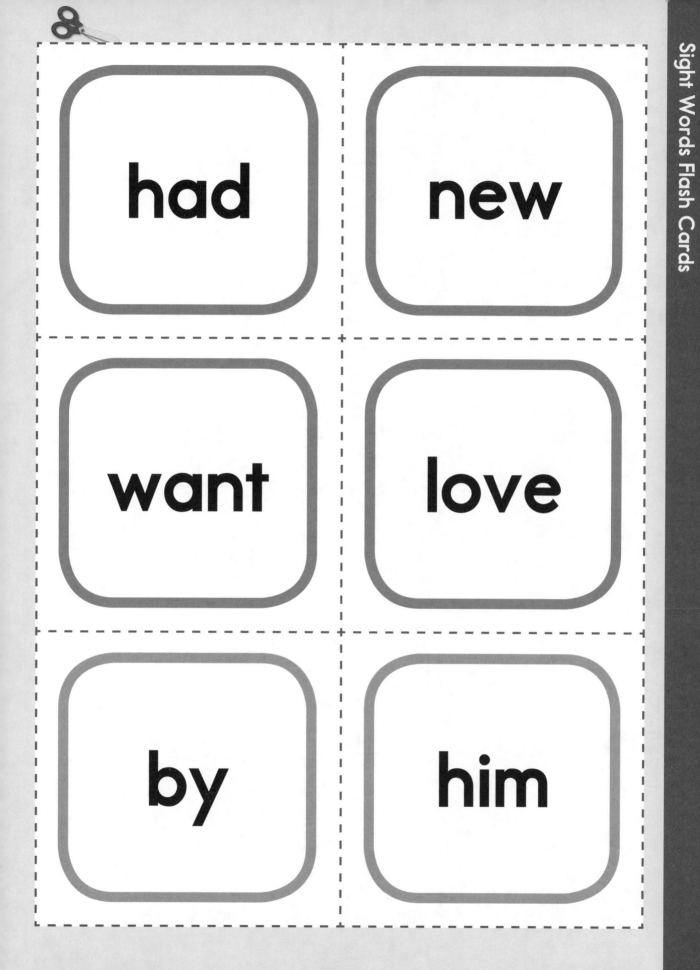

had

new

want

love

by

him

her

his

hers

has

may

old

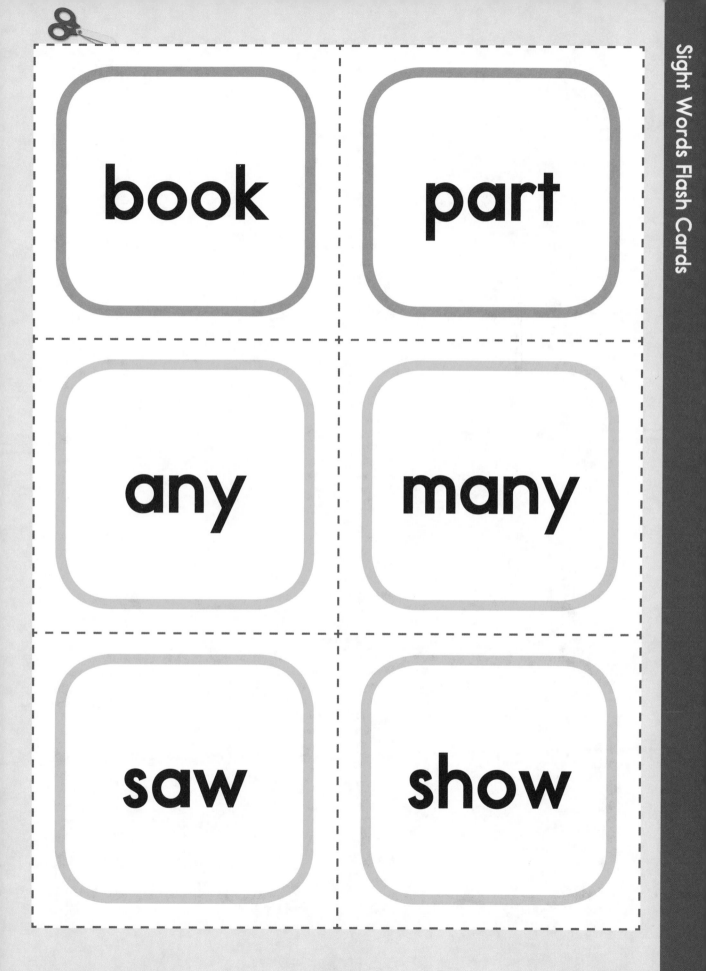

book

part

any

many

saw

show

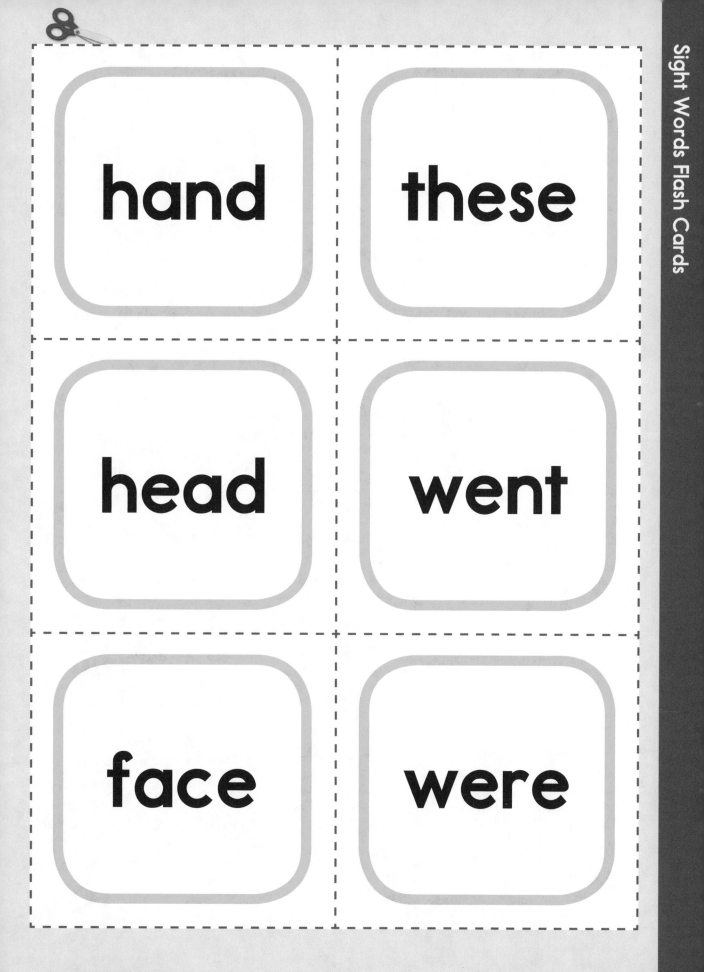

hand

these

head

went

face

were

next

walk

left

over

done

live

been

shoe

going

house

ask

how

who

then

when

what

them

name

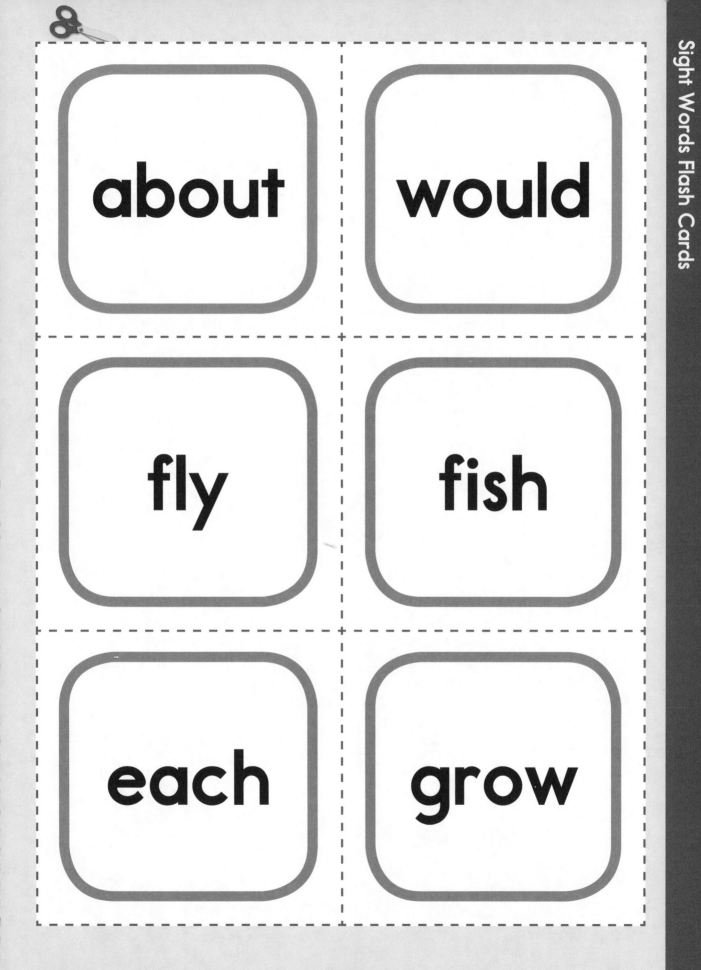

about

would

fly

fish

each

grow

small

some

take

water

under

round

wish

open

from

give

thank

happy

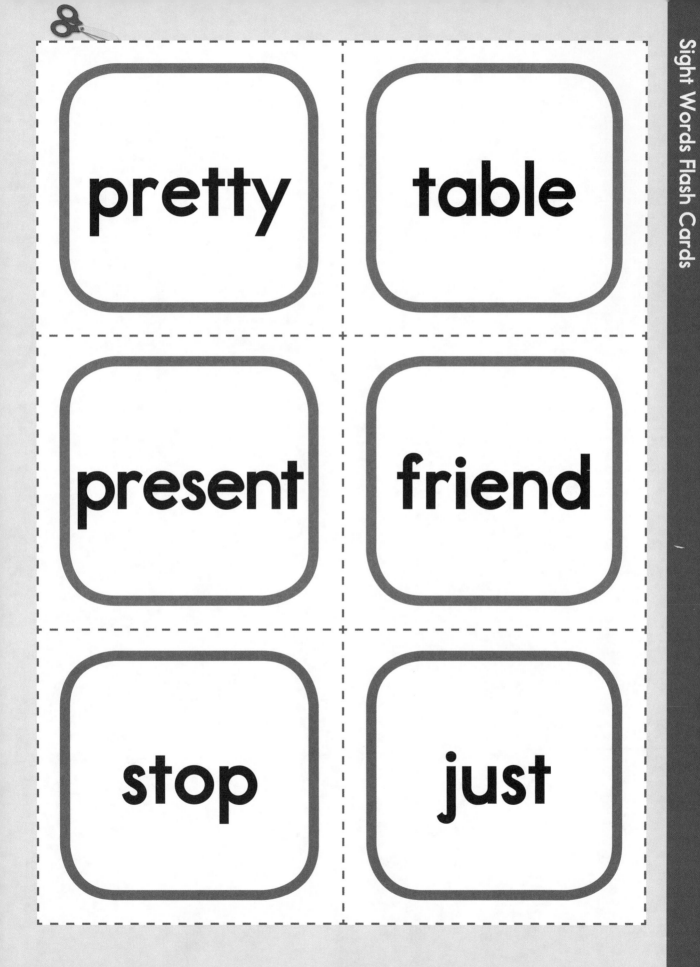

pretty

table

present

friend

stop

just

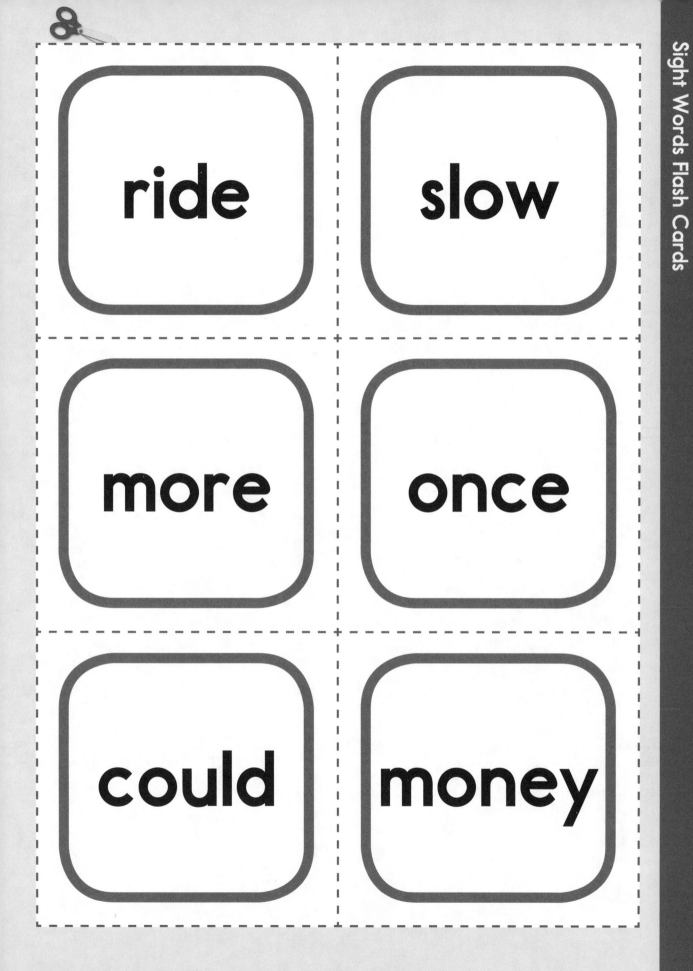

ride

slow

more

once

could

money

every

leave

now

last

time

soon

after

again

today

second

night

morning

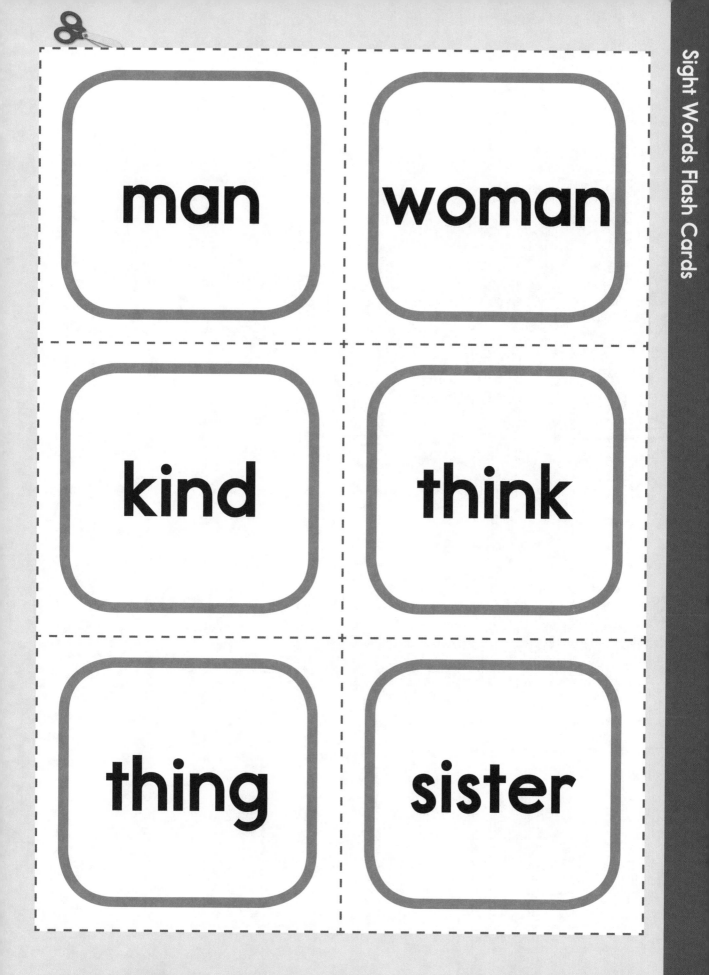

man

woman

kind

think

thing

sister

brother

should

please

know

Words with 7 Letters

Words with 6 Letters

Words with 5 Letters

Words with 4 Letters

Words with 3 Letters

Words with 2 Letters

REALLY GREAT READER!

Name _____

Can read 100 words!